D1743937

Have fun with
ORIGAMI

Look·in

Have fun with
ORIGAMI
ROBERT HARBIN

Illustrated by Keith Jones

Look-in

Independent Television Books Limited, London

INDEPENDENT TELEVISION BOOKS LTD.
247 Tottenham Court Road
London W1P 0AU

© Robert Harbin 1975

ISBN 0 900 72726 8

Printed in Great Britain by
Tinling (1973) Ltd., Prescot, Merseyside
(a member of the Oxley Printing Group Ltd.)

CONTENTS

BEFORE YOU START!

Origami is a Japanese word for paper-folding. Origami has now become a world-wide pastime and it appeals to all ages. All that is needed is a little patience and a little concentration.

You need have very little worry about the paper you are to use, almost any paper will do as long as it is thin and strong. For the most attractive results of course you can't beat real Origami paper which is brightly coloured on one side only and cut to size.

When I say 'cut to size', this is very important. If you are using a square of paper it must be exactly a square. If a rectangle, a perfect rectangle. An inaccurate square will make an imperfect model, as would an imperfect rectangle.

You can fold best when sitting at a table, or in a chair with a tray in your lap, or on the floor with a book to fold on . . . in other words always try to find a firm surface on which to fold for best results.

When you become expert you will find that you will be able to fold 'in the air' . . . sitting in a bus, or train . . . or even as you walk along . . .

In this book you will find a collection of prize-winning models, all originated by young readers of *Look-in*, junior TVTimes. When you start folding them I think you will agree that some of them are very ingenious indeed, and you will then be tempted to try to invent something of your very own.

Start folding now, but before you do make sure that you understand the symbols and terms and just what Origami is all about.

SYMBOLS

A brief word about the symbols. On pages 8 and 9 you will see the various signs or symbols which have been used by the artist to help you with the folds.

These symbols are universal and it is possible that you have already come across these in other Origami books.

It is essential that you remember what the symbols mean. All you need is about two minutes study of these pages. Whenever you are folding a model and you don't know what a symbol means, turn back to pages 8 and 9 and put yourself right.

You will notice that on pages 12 and 13 there are some illustrations showing you just what Squash Folds and Petal Folds are. These terms along with others are used a great deal in Origami and many times in this book. With this in mind, and in case you have not come across this hobby before, it is necessary for you to understand these two procedures.

When you have absorbed this little bit of knowledge you will be well equipped to tackle the paper-folds in this book.

SYMBOLS

Valley fold (dashes)

Mountain fold (dashes and dots)

So with arrows and symbols this is the result

Dots indicate X-ray view

Creases look like this

This circle means hold

This star means follow the star

This arrow says fold in front (see above)

This arrow says fold behind

8

SYMBOLS

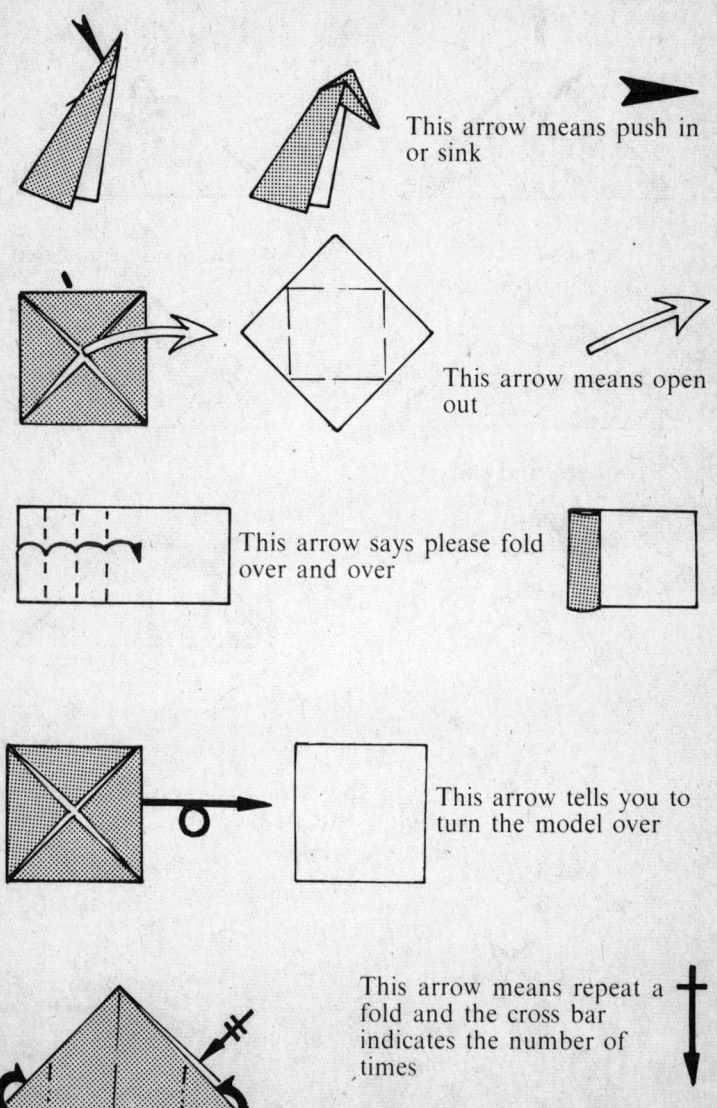

This arrow means push in or sink

This arrow means open out

This arrow says please fold over and over

This arrow tells you to turn the model over

This arrow means repeat a fold and the cross bar indicates the number of times

9

PROCEDURES

1 The sink arrow plus the crease arrow tell you to

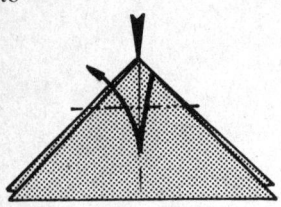

2 Crease in front

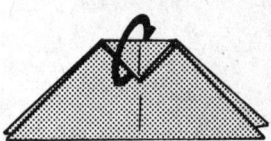

3 Then behind

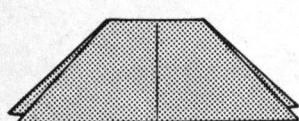

4 Hold sides indicated

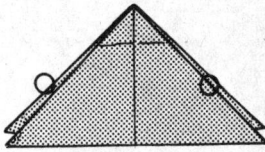

5 Stretch and sink

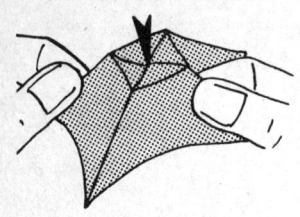

6 So

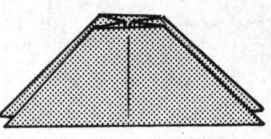

7 The sink arrow plus these other symbols indicate a crimp

8 So

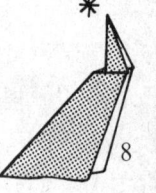

9 Or an outside crimp like this

10 So

10

PROCEDURES

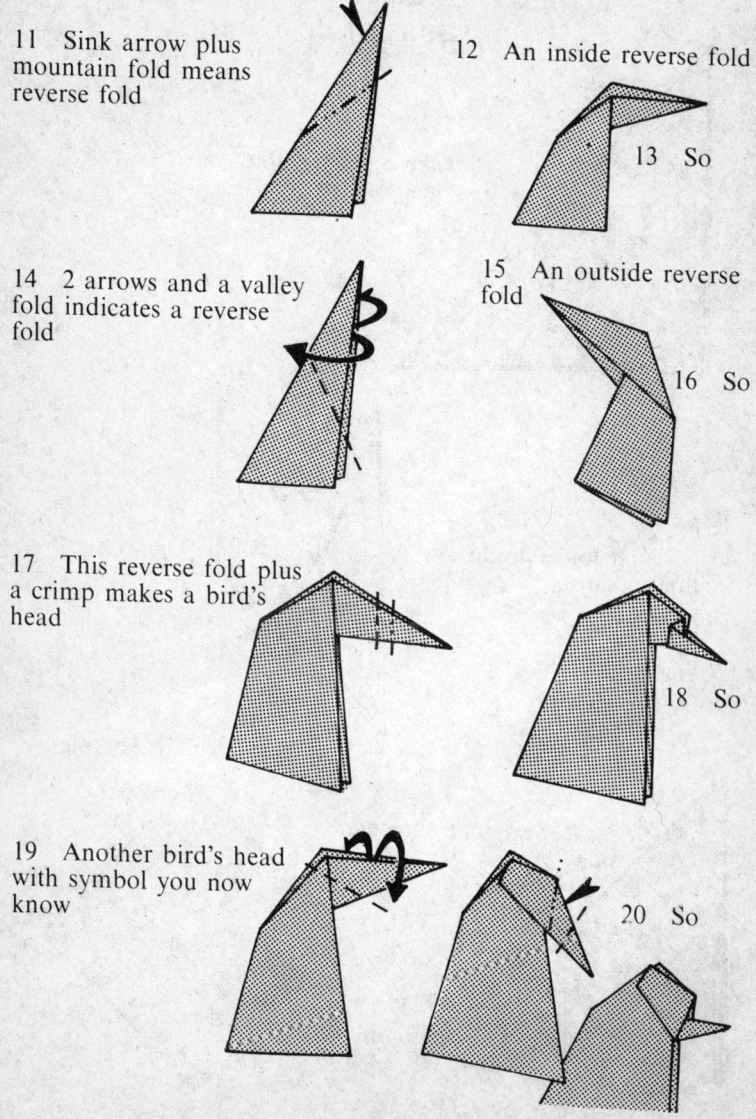

11 Sink arrow plus mountain fold means reverse fold

12 An inside reverse fold

13 So

14 2 arrows and a valley fold indicates a reverse fold

15 An outside reverse fold

16 So

17 This reverse fold plus a crimp makes a bird's head

18 So

19 Another bird's head with symbol you now know

20 So

SQUASH FOLD
These symbols indicate a squash fold

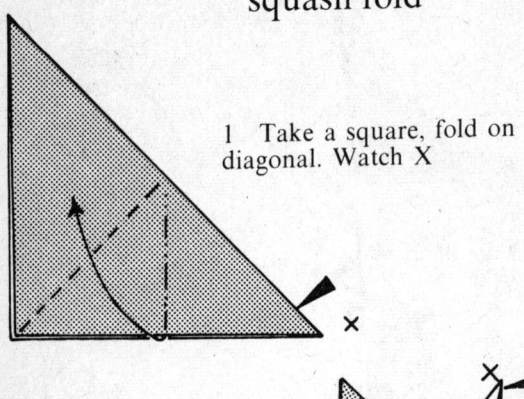

1 Take a square, fold on diagonal. Watch X

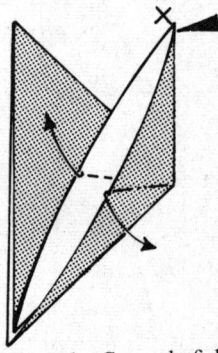

2 First fold upright and then open up sides and squash

4 Squash folds complete

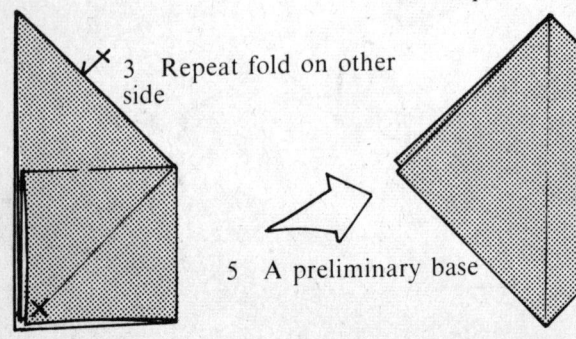

3 Repeat fold on other side

5 A preliminary base

PETAL FOLD
These symbols
indicate a
petal fold

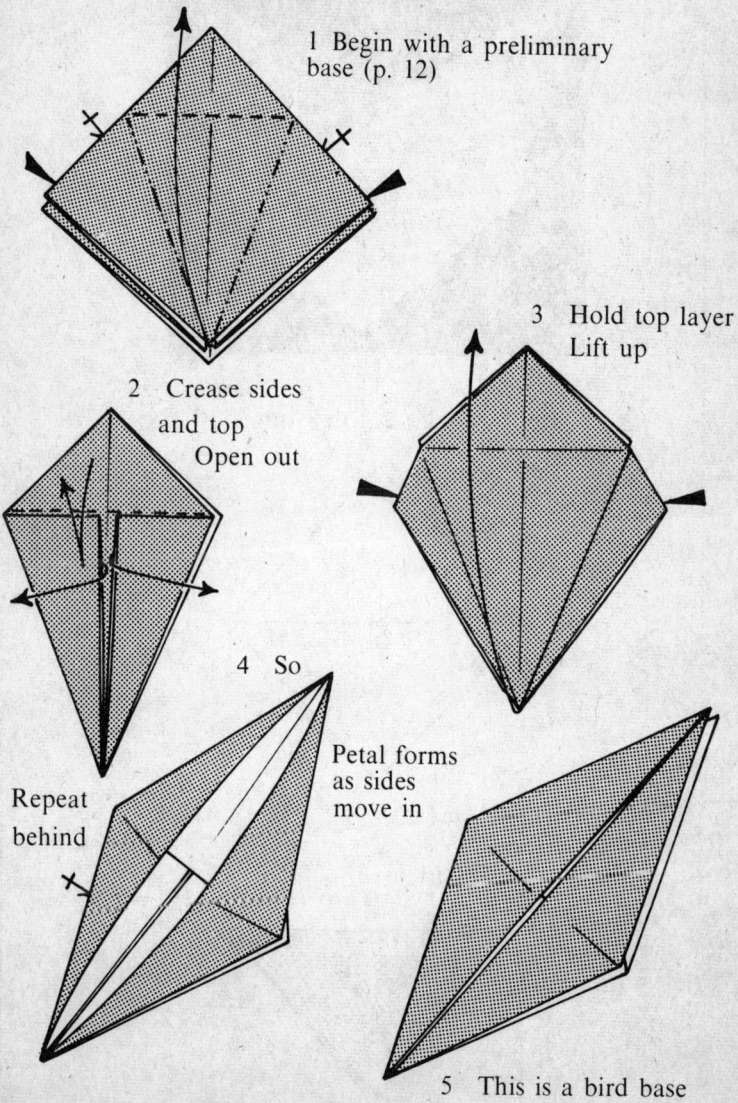

1 Begin with a preliminary base (p. 12)

2 Crease sides and top Open out

3 Hold top layer Lift up

4 So

Petal forms as sides move in

Repeat behind

5 This is a bird base

CAT
by Danille Wishnie (London)

1
Fold a square along diagonal

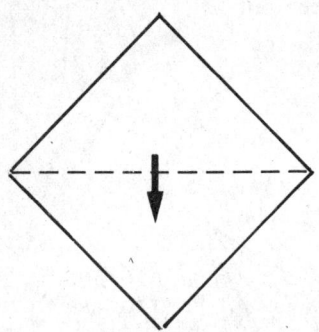

2
Fold corners in

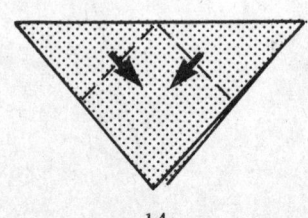

14

3
Fold corners up

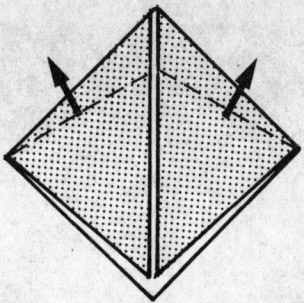

4
Fold top flap down and
bottom flap up

5
Draw the eyes

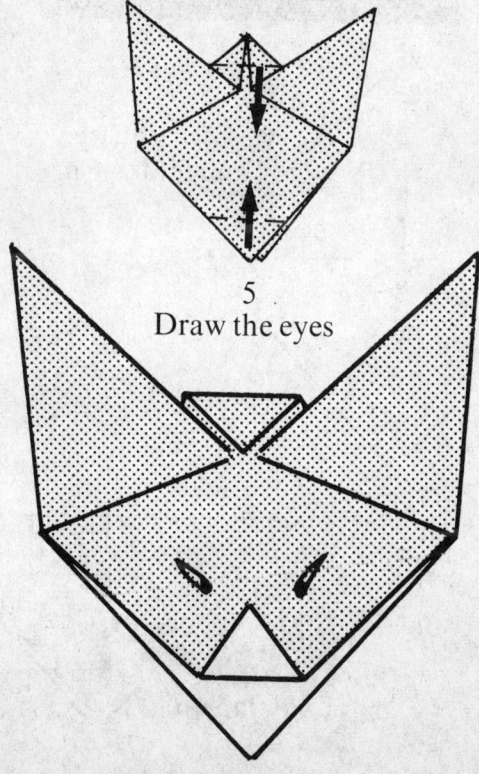

PEKINESE
by Sally Gittler

1
Crease a square
and fold down

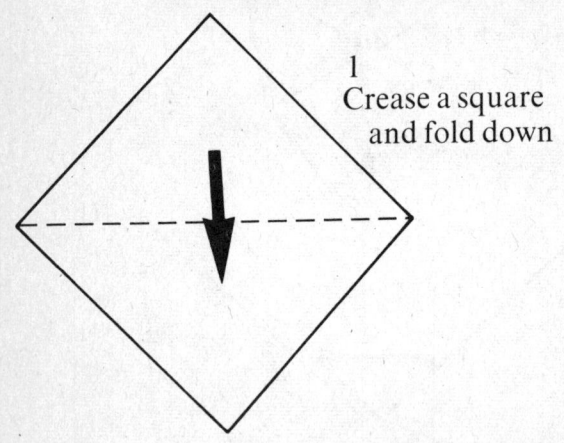

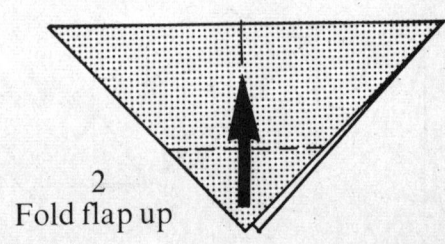

2
Fold flap up

3
Fold top flap down,
fold under flap up

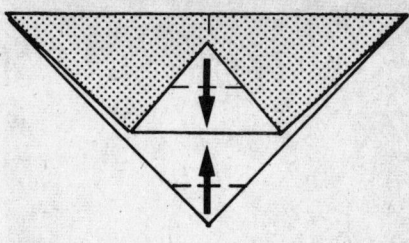

4
Fold the ears

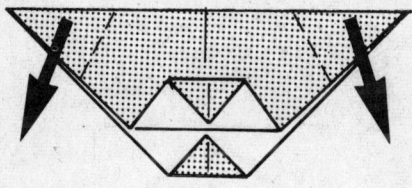

5
Draw the eyes

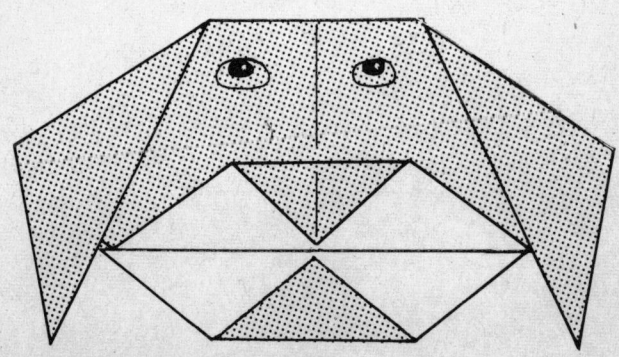

PIG
by Terry Ann (Acton)

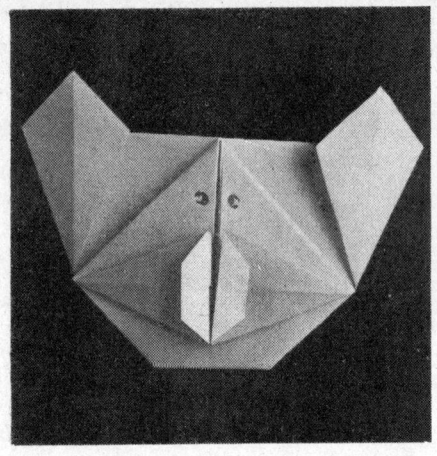

1

Crease a square to make
water bomb base

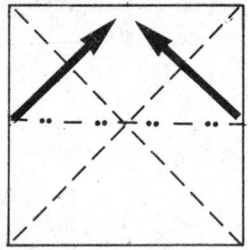

2

Fold corner behind

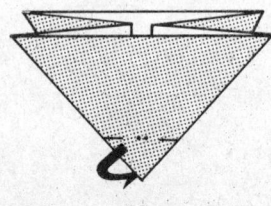

3
Fold front points down

4
Lift points and squash

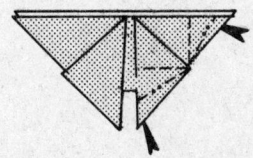

5
Squash other 2 points

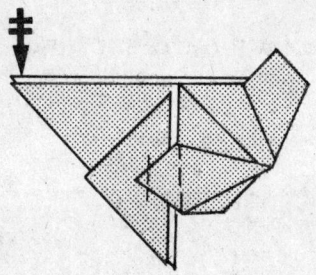

6
Fold tip twice

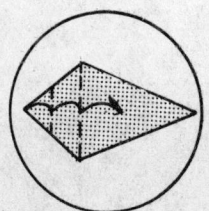 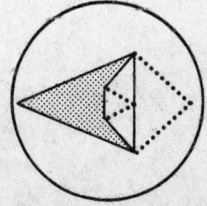

PIG (cont.)

7

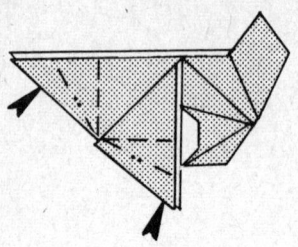

8
Draw the eyes and nose

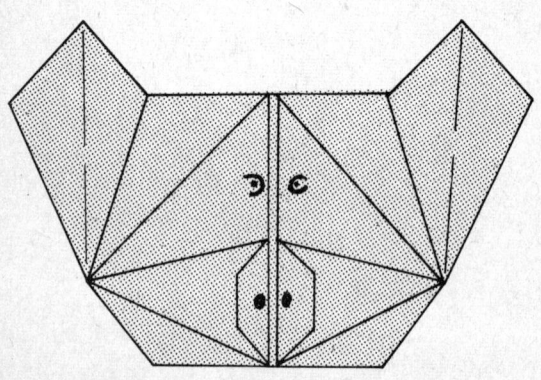

SNAKE
by Mark Taylor (Windsor)

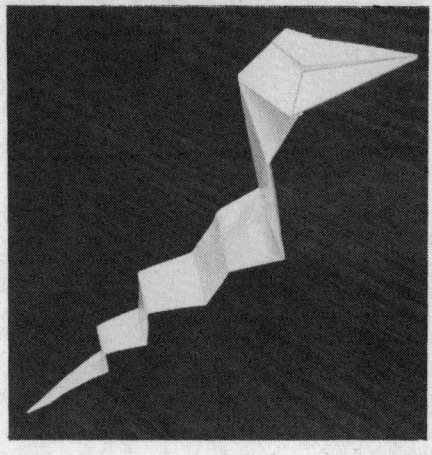

1

Take a square and fold sides in

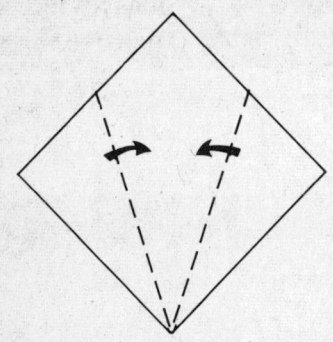

2

Fold again

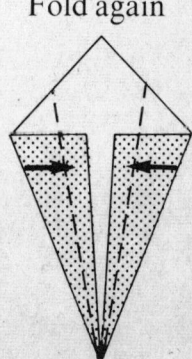

SNAKE (cont.)

3
And again

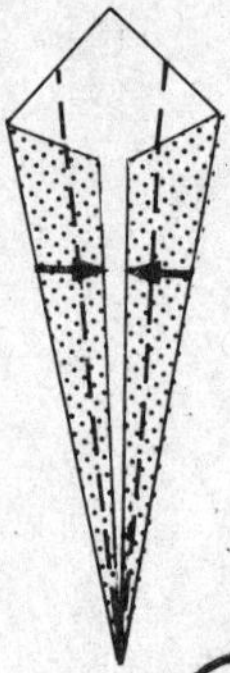

4
Turn over

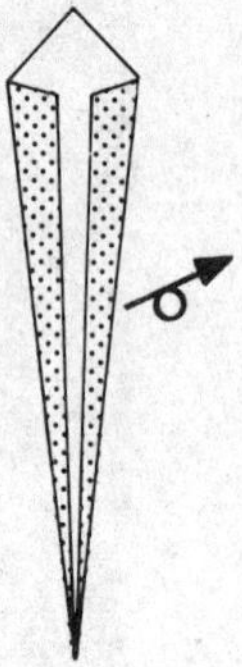

5
Crease body
of snake

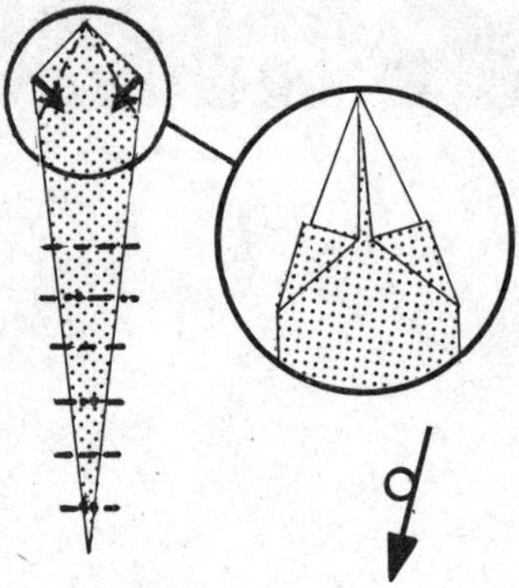

6
Sides folded in.
Turn over

7
Fold down

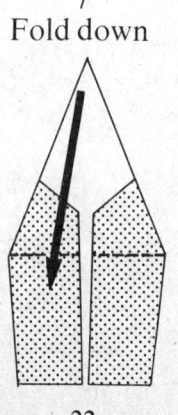

8
Sink corners

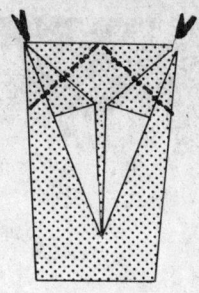

9
So

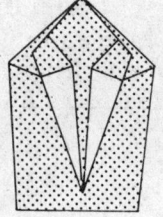

10

RABBIT
by Shelley Mitchen

1
Take a rectangle, preferably 10 × 18cm.
Crease valley along dashes,
then turn over

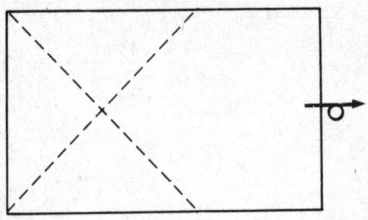

2
Crease again.
Then turn over

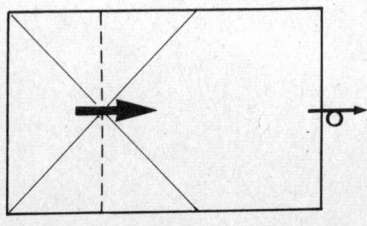

3
Fold creases in
A and B meet

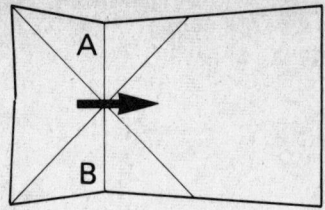

4
Fold centre down, fold front flaps up

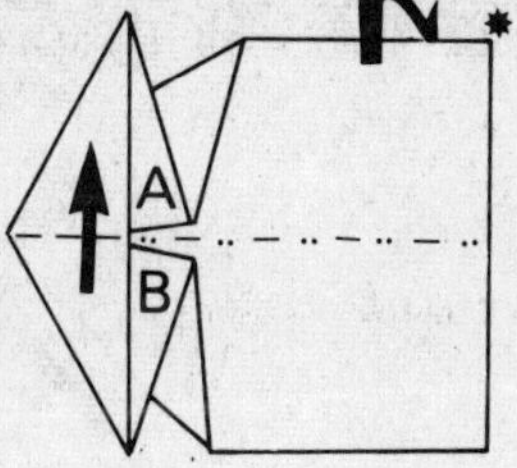

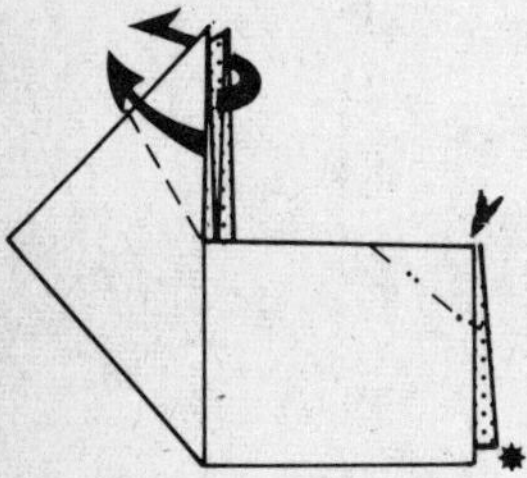

5
Fold ears
Push tail in

6
Draw the eyes

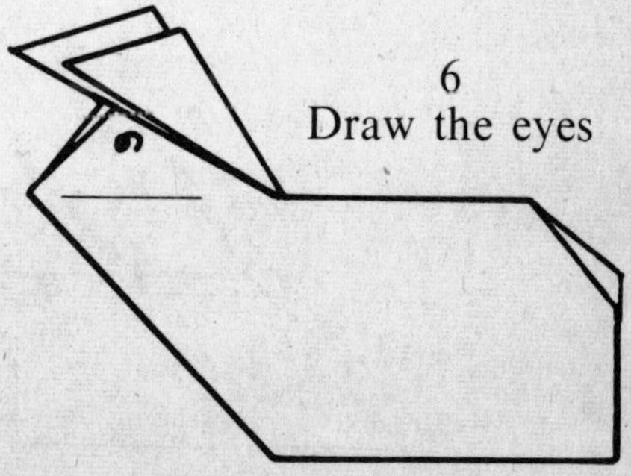

DOG
by Denise Bacon (Crowborough)

1
Fold a square in half.
Fold corner down

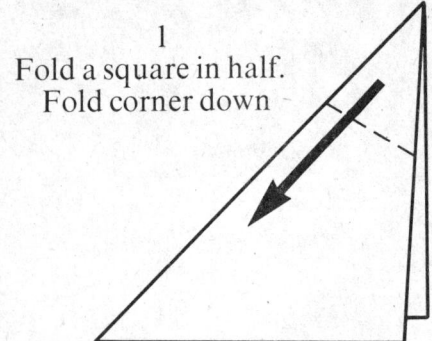

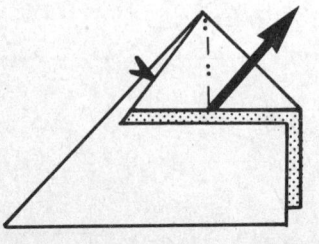

2
Squash fold

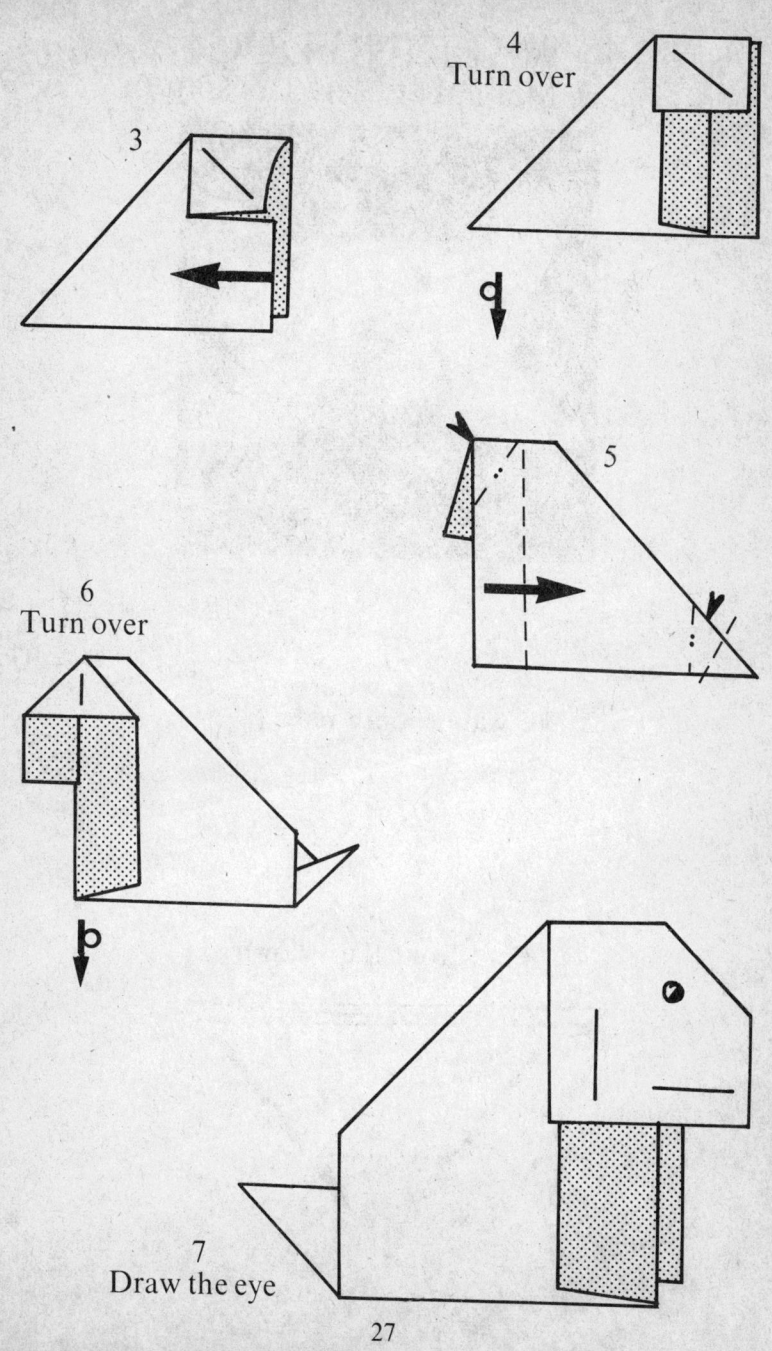

3

4
Turn over

5

6
Turn over

7
Draw the eye

27

WALKING DOG
by Margaret Fegen (Paisley)

1
Take a square.
Make water bomb base (p. 18)

2
Fold front flaps down

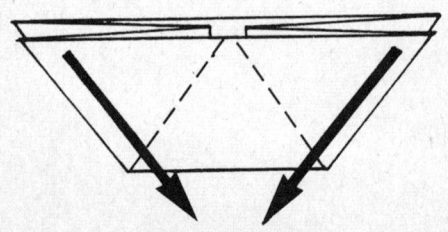

3
Fold corners behind

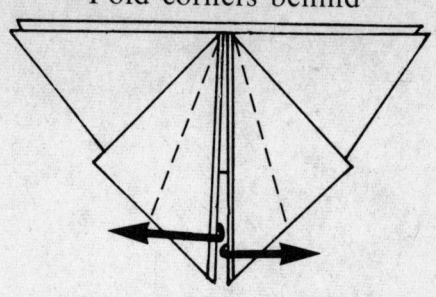

4
Squash fold head

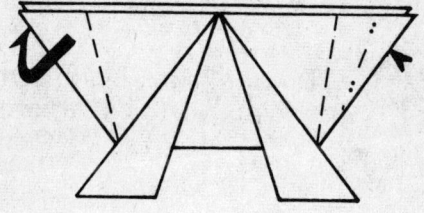

5
Draw the face

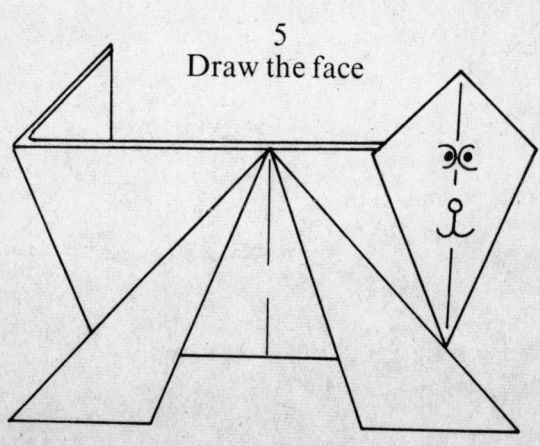

TADPOLE
by Richard Hubbard (London)

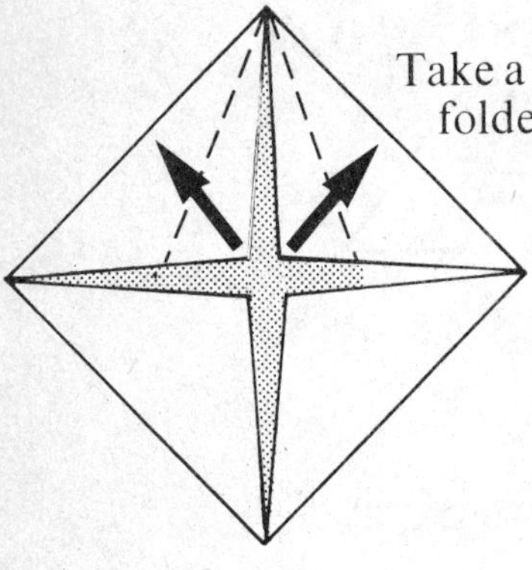

1

Take a square. Begin with corners folded in, fold two corners back

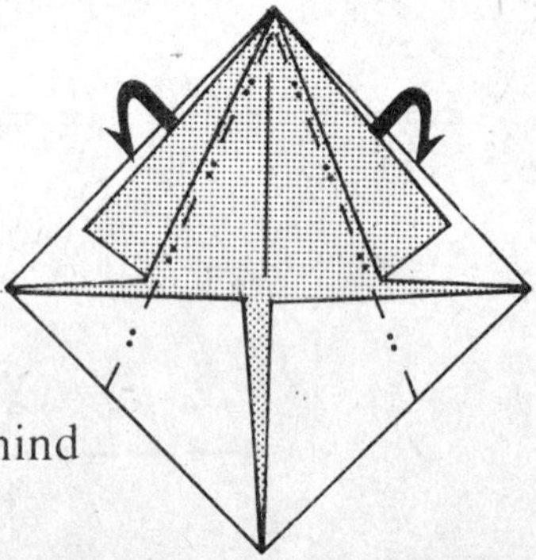

2
Fold flaps behind

3
Fold in half

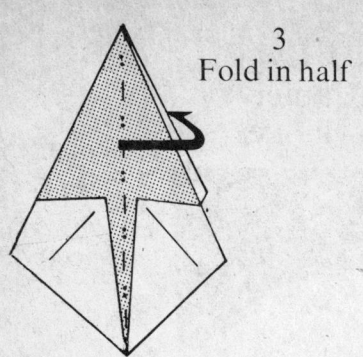

4
Reverse fold head and tail

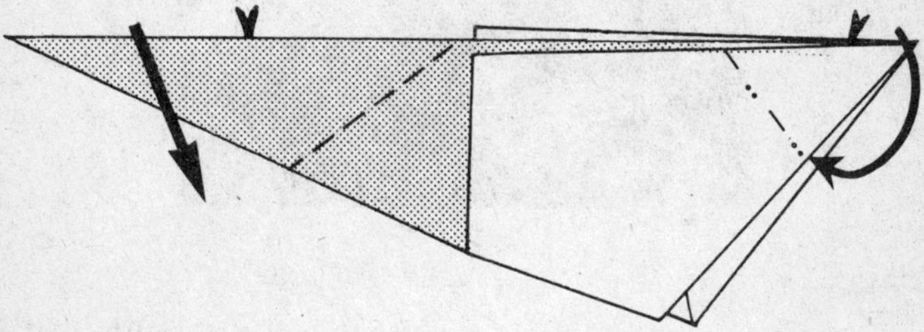

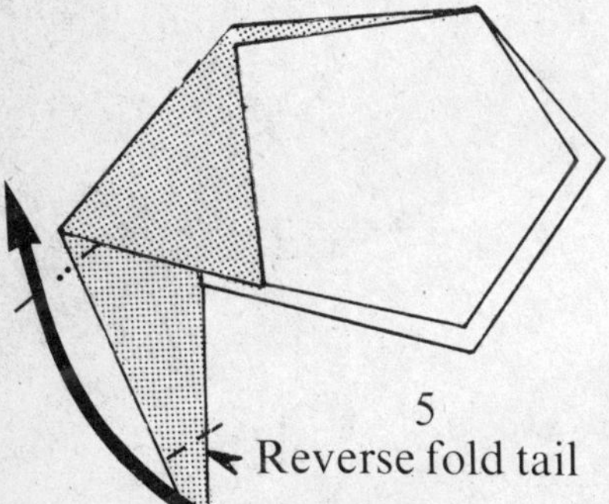

5
Reverse fold tail

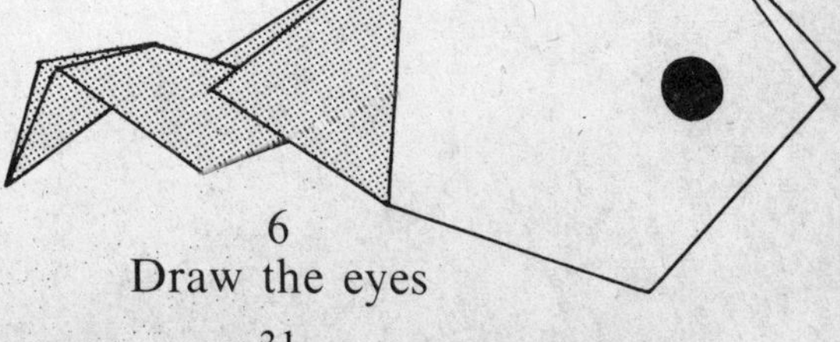

6
Draw the eyes

31

FLYING FISH
by Robert Mather
(Henley-on-Thames)

1
Take a square and fold as illustration. Fold flap behind

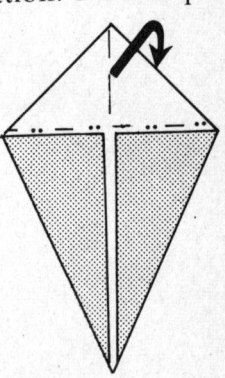

2
Fold corners forward

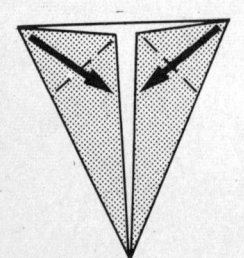

3
Pull A and B out to form fins

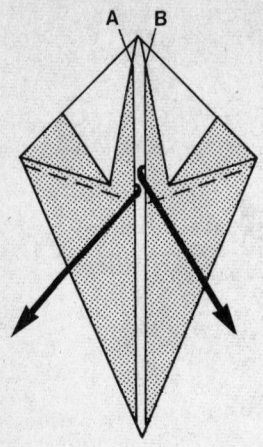

4
Fold in half

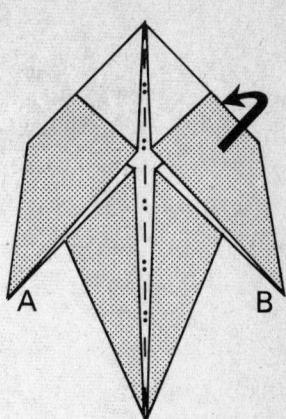

5
Sink nose and tail

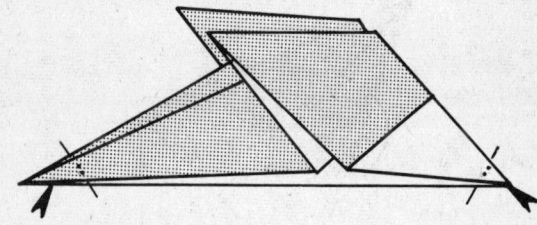

6
Draw the eyes

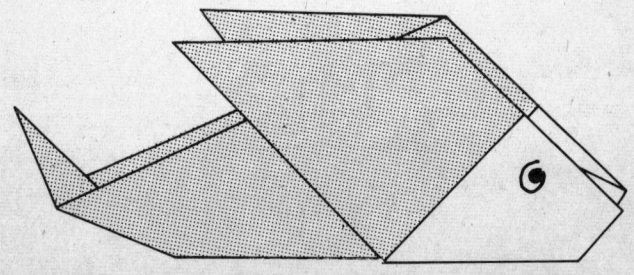

WHALE
by Robert Harbin

1
Take a square. Fold as illustration

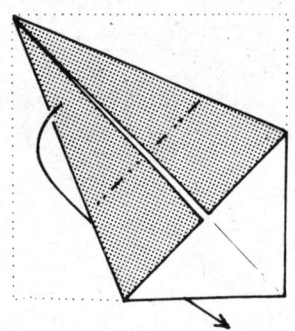

2

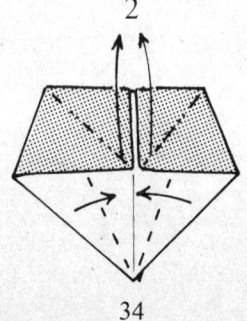

3

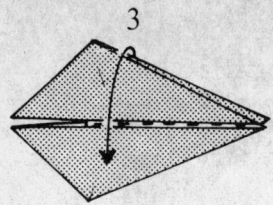

4
Fold points in as indicated

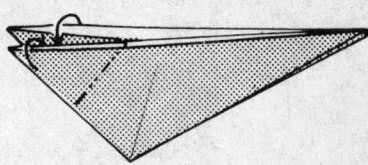

5
Reverse fold tail

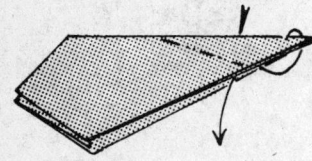

6
Fold long flaps into body

7
Reverse fold again

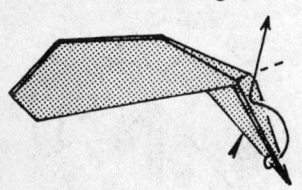

8
Reverse fold inside point

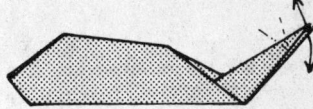

9

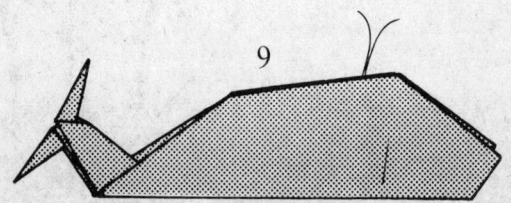

JAPANESE CICADA
(Singing Beetle)

1
Fold a square in half.
Fold the 2 corners in

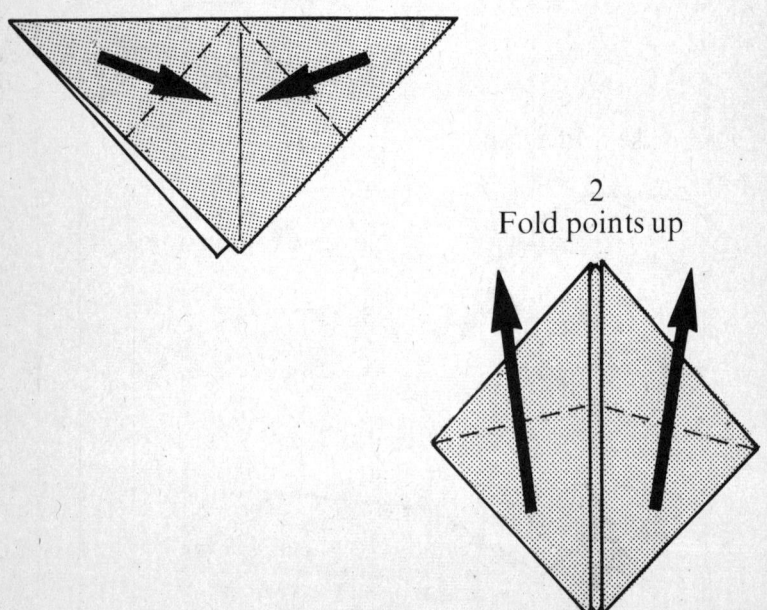

2
Fold points up

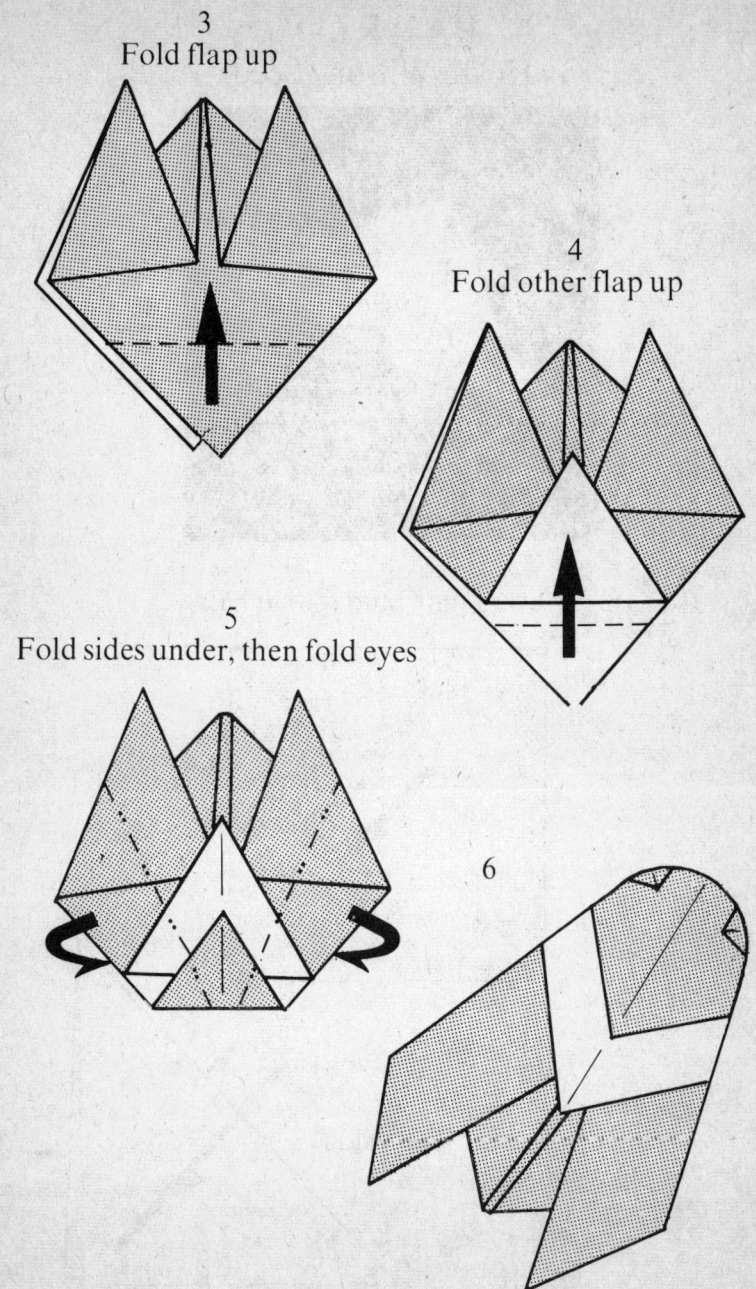

3
Fold flap up

4
Fold other flap up

5
Fold sides under, then fold eyes

6

37

PARROT
by Kevin Wilson (Leeds)

1
Take a square and fold in half

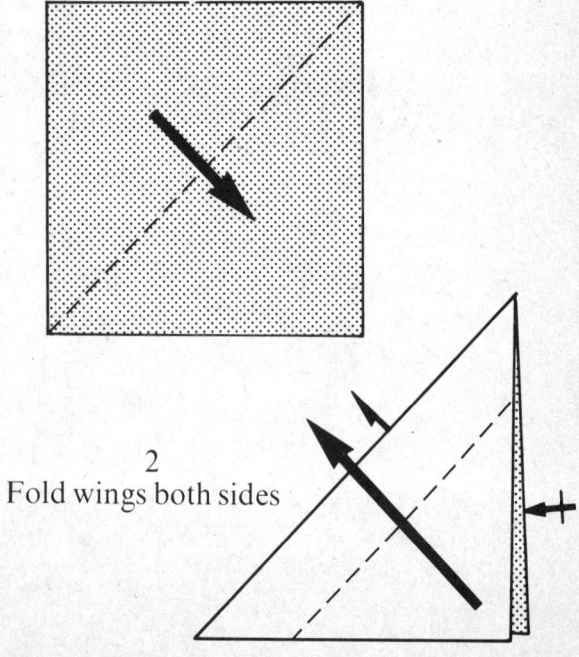

2
Fold wings both sides

3
Reverse fold head.
Fold tail flaps in

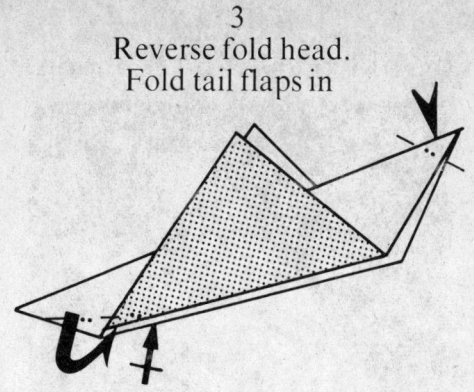

4
Fold head flaps in

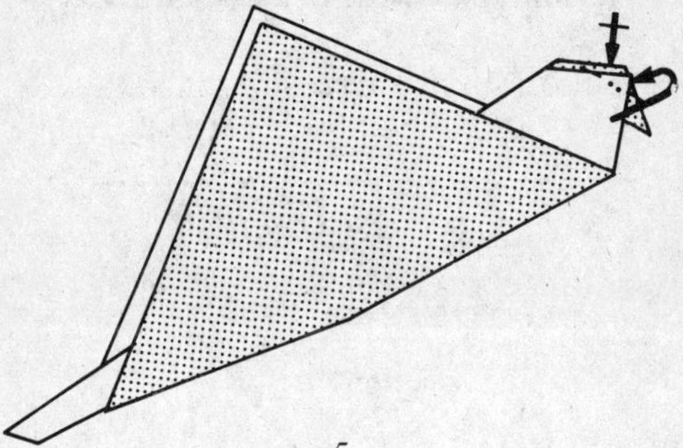

5

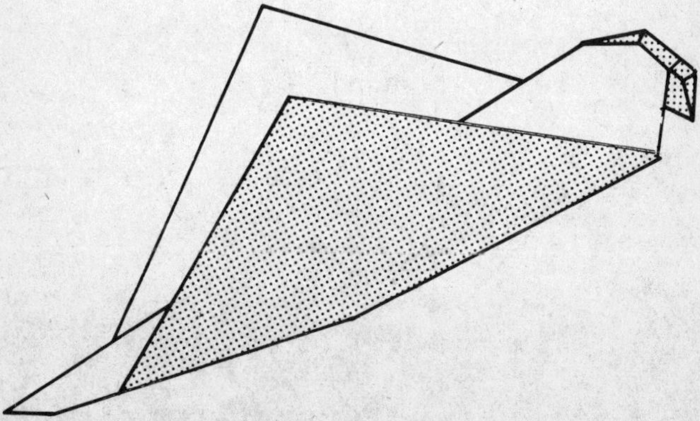

BIRD
by Gideon Ovadia (London)

1
Take a square. Crease 2 diagonals.
Fold in half. Fold flap up

2
Fold in half

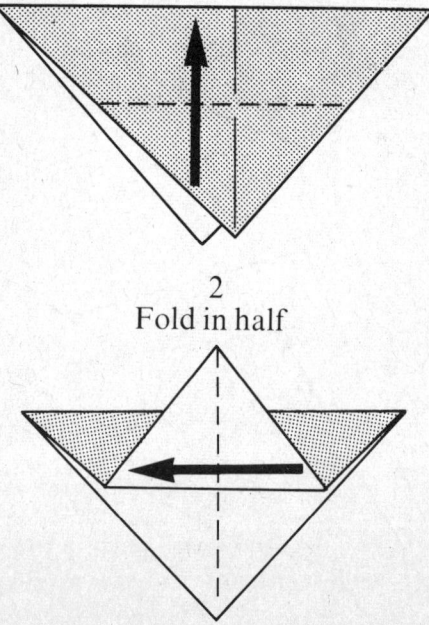

3
Fold wings both sides and watch*

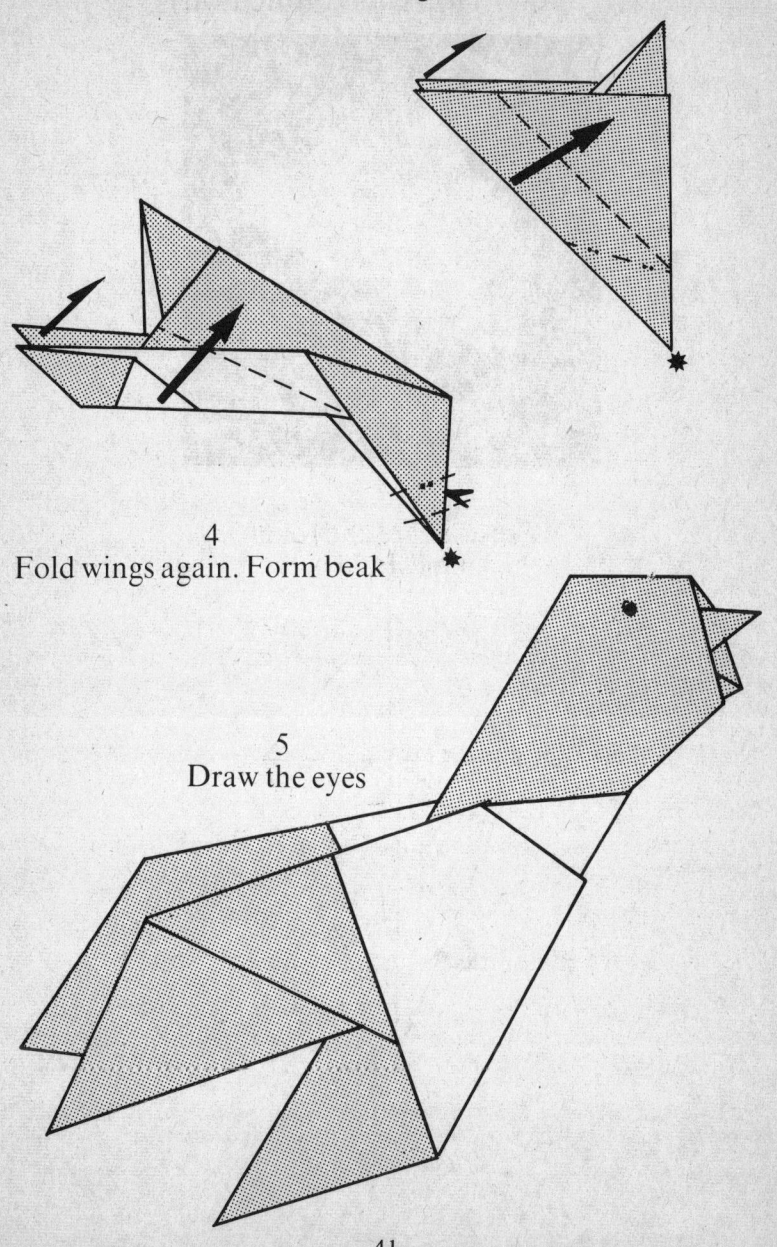

4
Fold wings again. Form beak

5
Draw the eyes

41

SWAN
by Peter Hopkins (Nuneaton)

1

Take a square and fold to
this shape. Fold behind

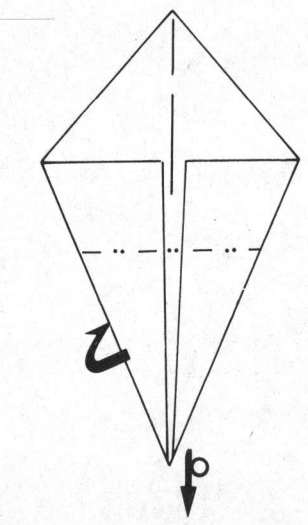

2
Crease and push in

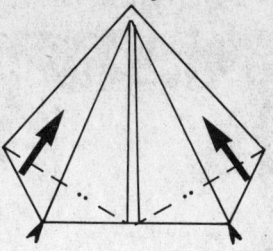

3
Fold big flap only behind and fold front flaps

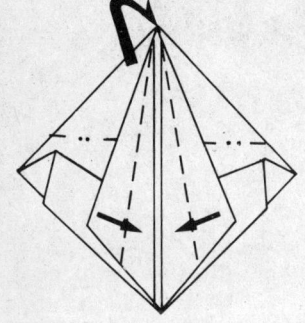

4
Fold neck in front, body behind

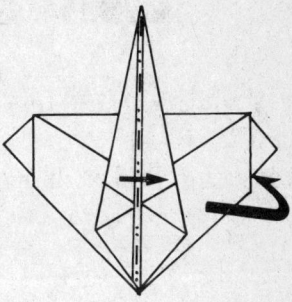

5
Shape neck and note how head is made

6

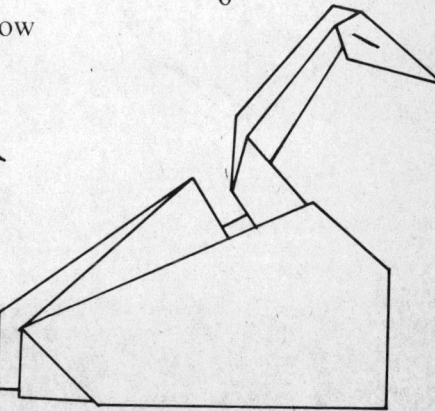

43

OWL
by Howard Winik (Liverpool)

You need 2 squares

1
Crease and fold each piece

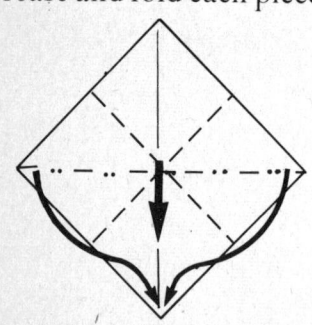

2
Make 2 preliminary bases

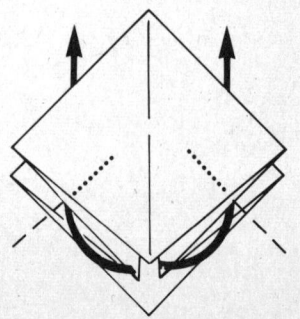

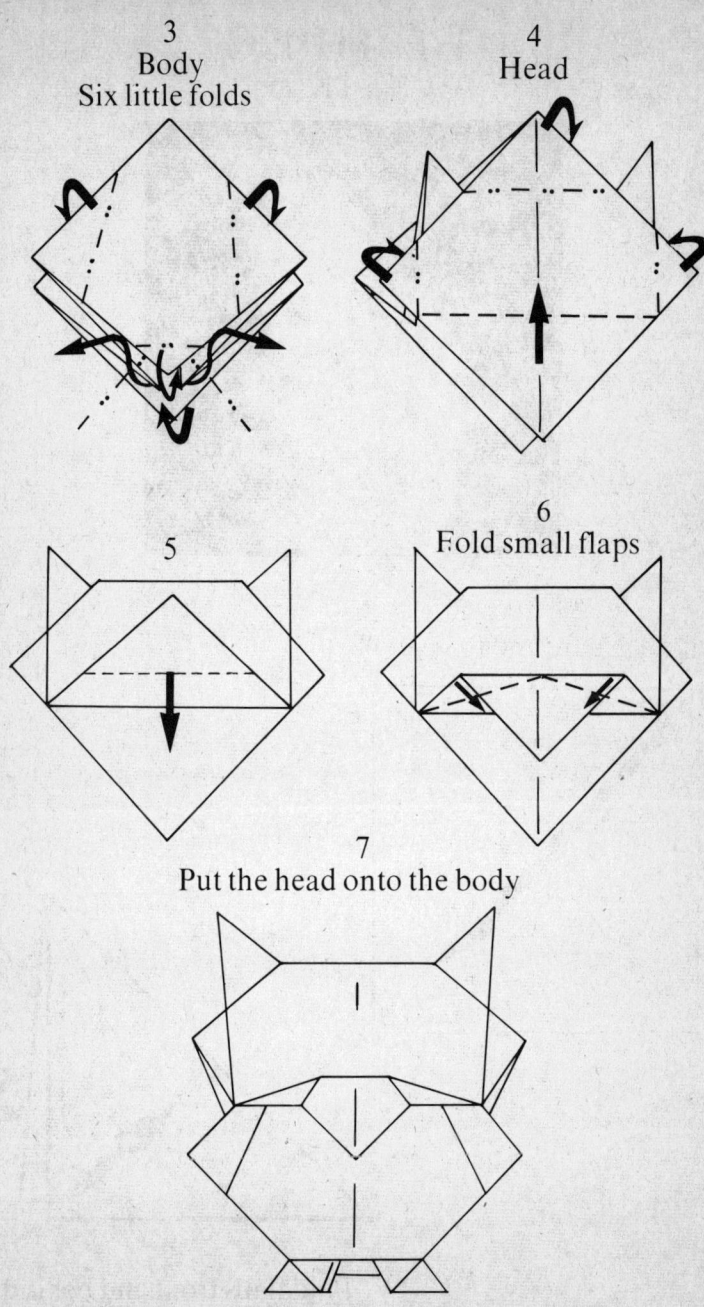

3
Body
Six little folds

4
Head

5

6
Fold small flaps

7
Put the head onto the body

45

THE 'THING'
by Karl Kops

1
Take a square and fold A to B

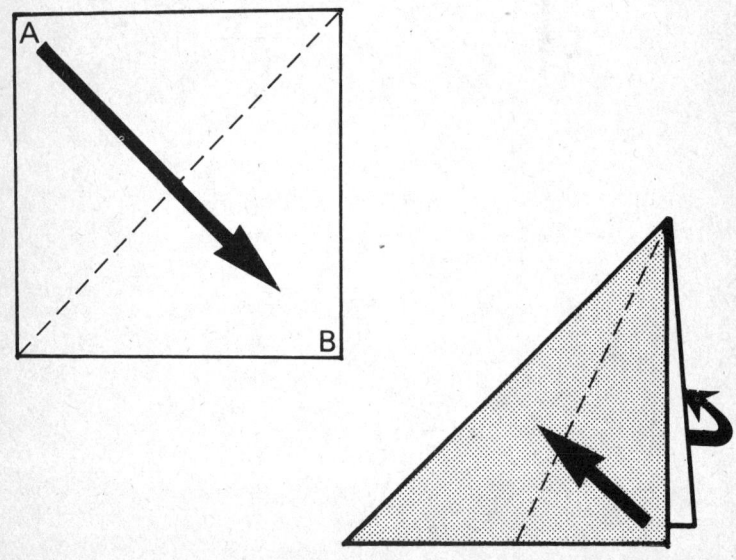

2
Fold flaps front and behind

46

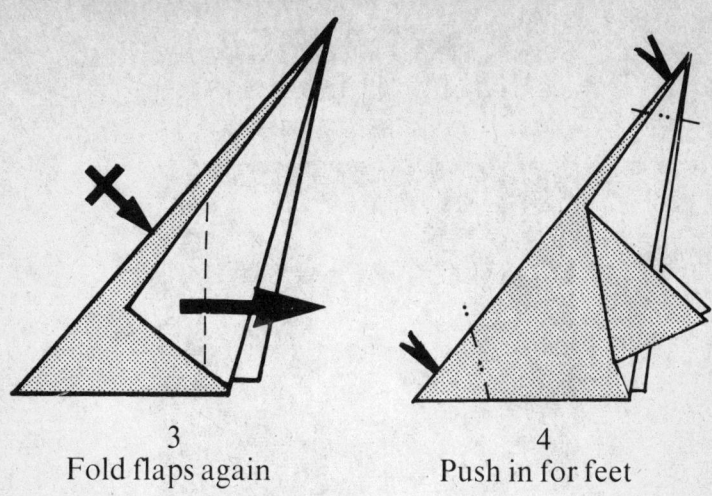

3
Fold flaps again

4
Push in for feet

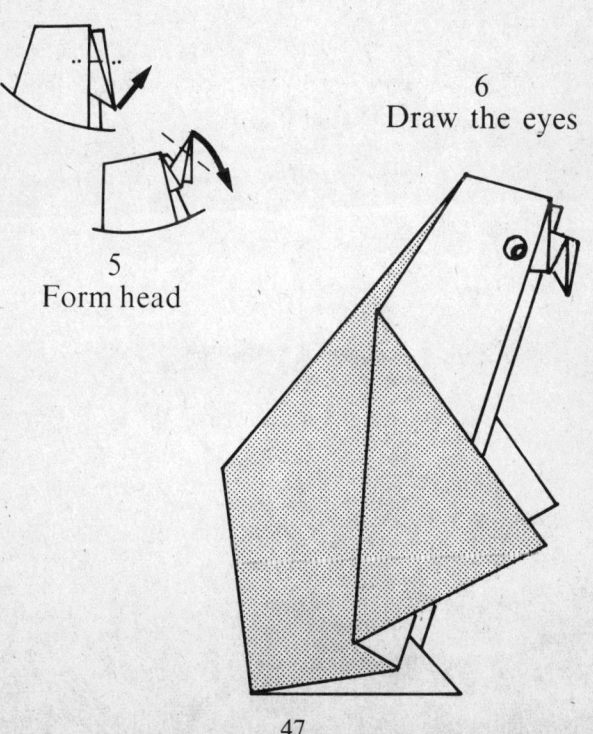

5
Form head

6
Draw the eyes

KINGFISHER
by Julian Humphreys
(Chessington)

1
Take a square, crease diagonal,
fold sides in

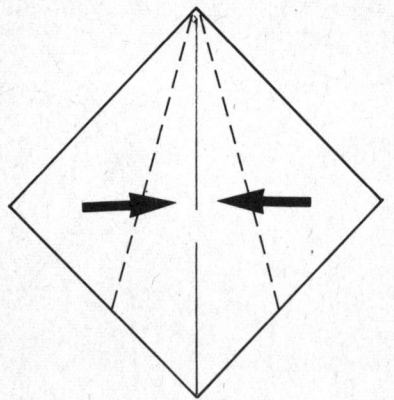

2
Fold flaps out

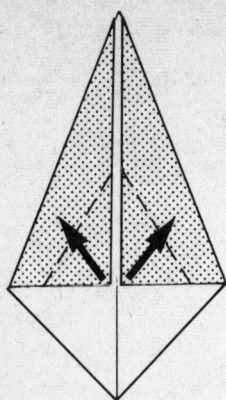

3
Fold head

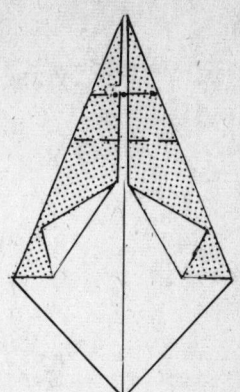

4
Now fold in half B to A

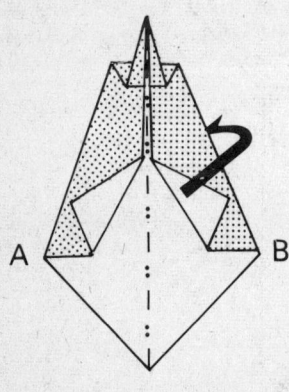

A   B

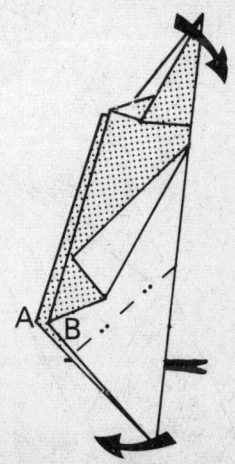

A B

5
Pull beak down. Reverse fold point

6
Reverse fold point again

7
Draw the eyes

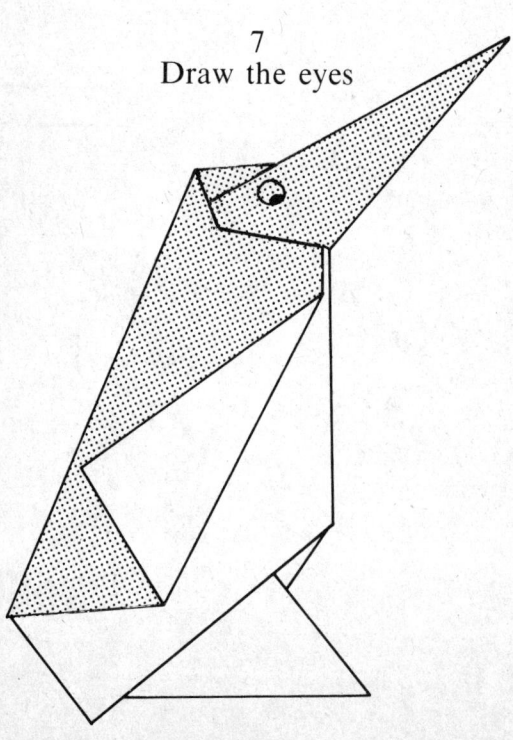

PENGUIN
by Mark Kelmanson

1

Fold a square along diagonal

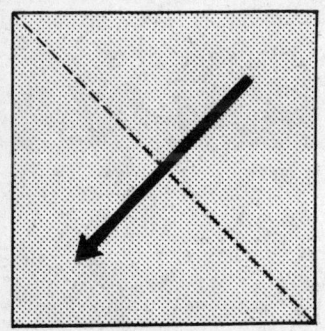

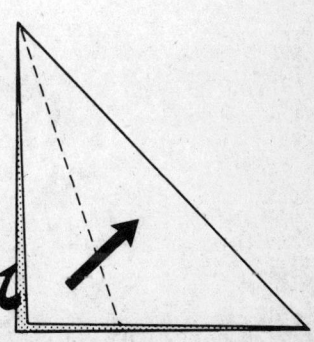

2

Fold flaps in front and behind

51

PENGUIN (cont.)

3
Fold flaps again in front and behind

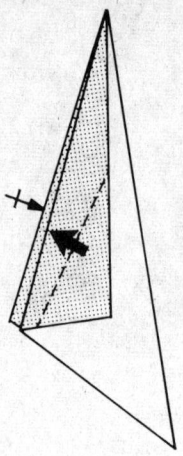

4
Fold flippers and crimp feet

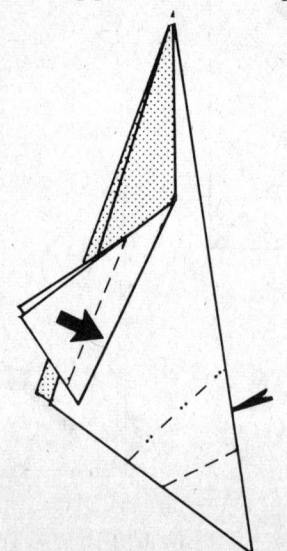

5
Reverse fold head, fold wings again. Fold feet

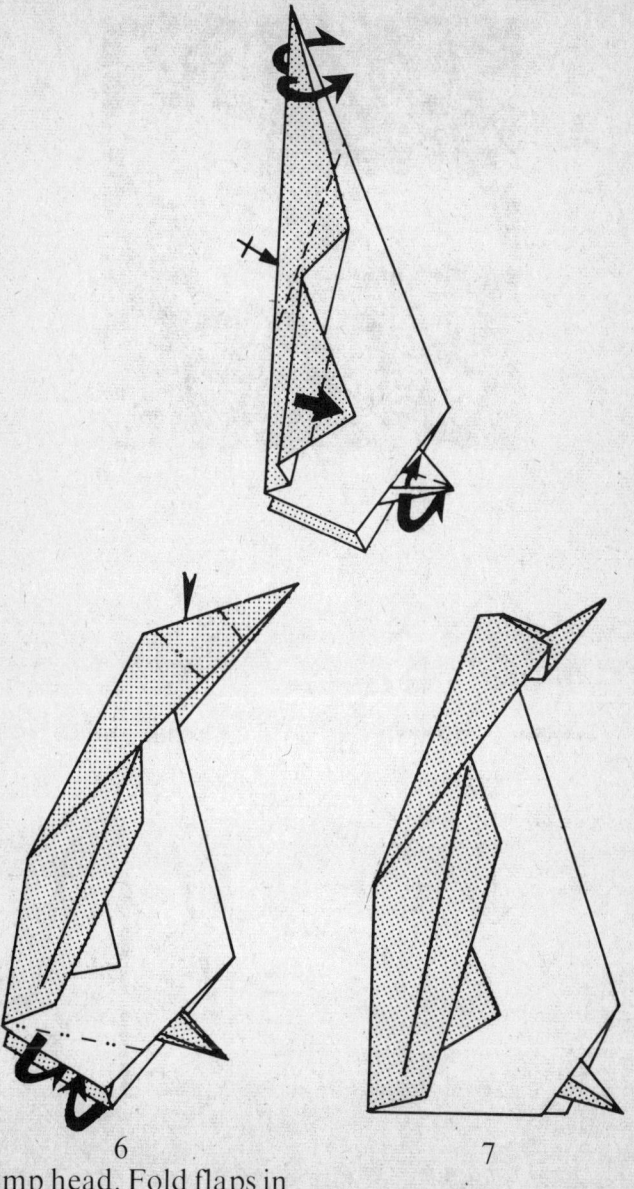

6
Crimp head. Fold flaps in

7

BOX 1
by Martin Moore (Surrey)

1
Crease a square, fold sides

2
Crease and fold

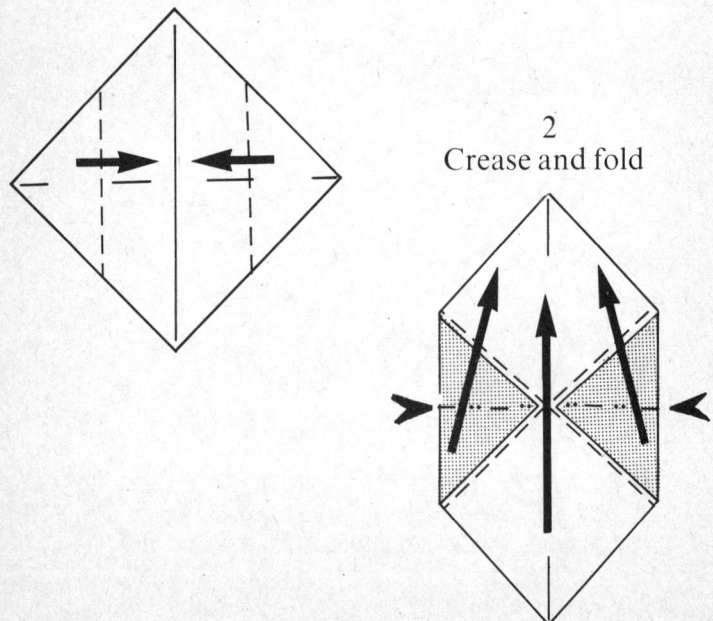

3
Fold sides in

4
Fold flaps down

5
Open out

6

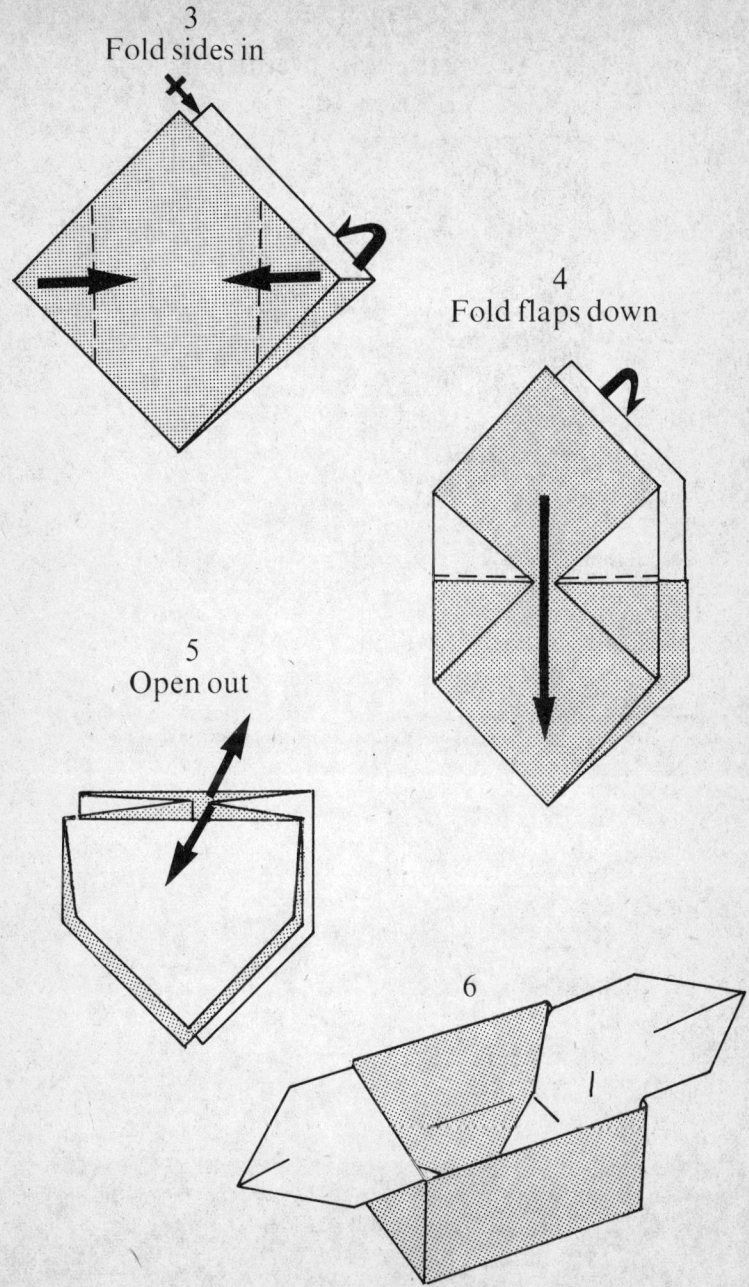

BOX 2
by John Richardson
(Doncaster)

1
Take a square, crease diagonals,
fold corners behind

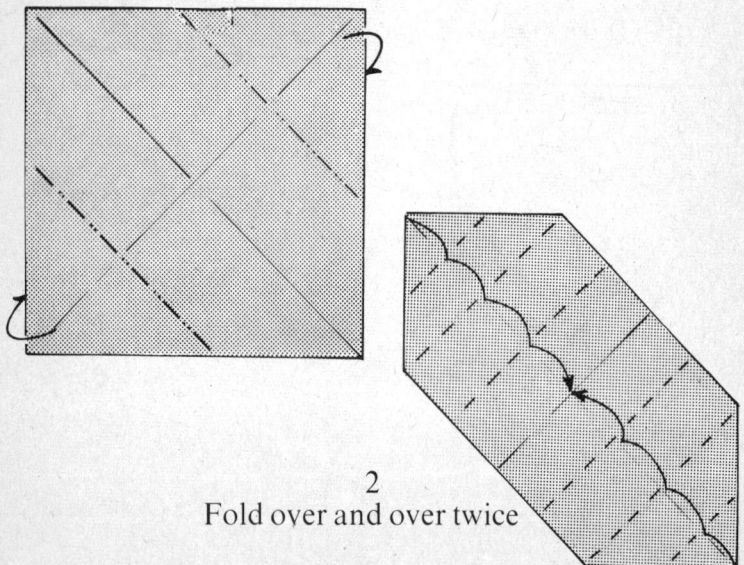

2
Fold over and over twice

3

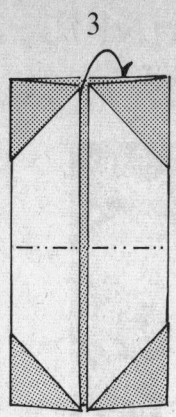

4
Open and fold

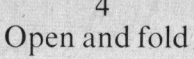

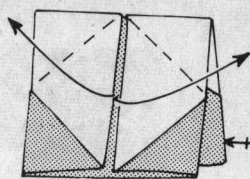

5
4 squash folds

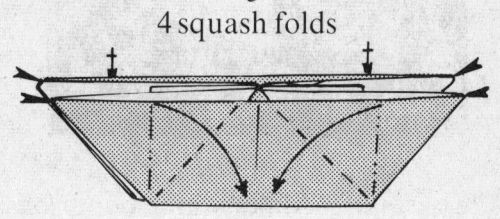

6
Tuck 4 flaps in

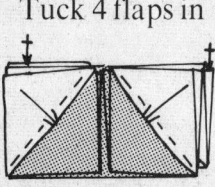

7

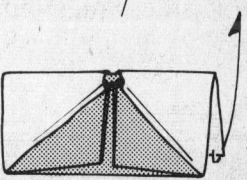

8
Open out, form box

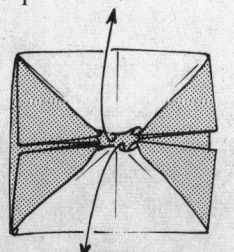

9

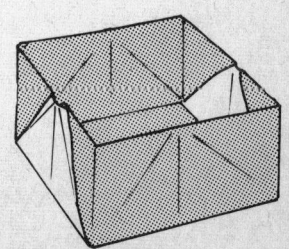

WATER CONTAINER
by John Richardson
(Doncaster)

1

Take a square. Make water bomb base
(p. 18)

Fold side, squash corners
front and back

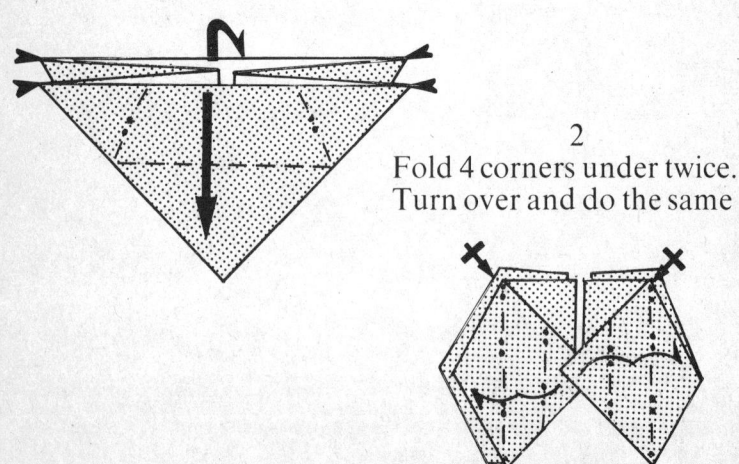

2

Fold 4 corners under twice.
Turn over and do the same

3
Swing sides front and behind

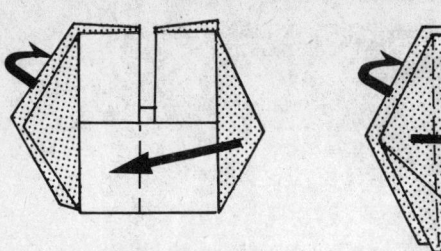

4
Fold 4 flaps

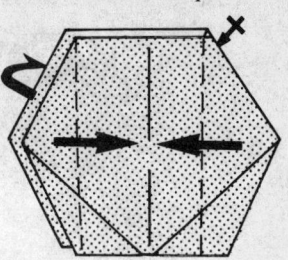

5
Fold sides down and open box out

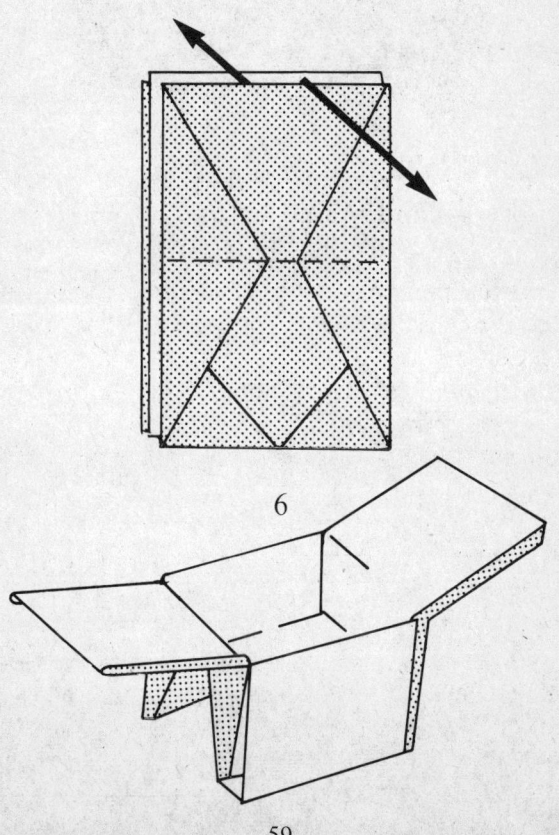

6

YACHT
by Laura Wilson
(Wolverhampton)

1
Take a square and crease. Fold flaps
in front and behind

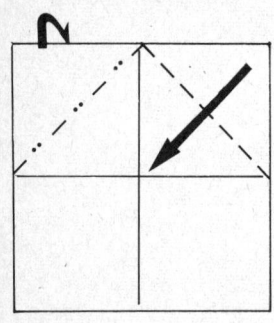

2
Fold flap

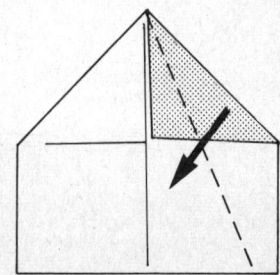

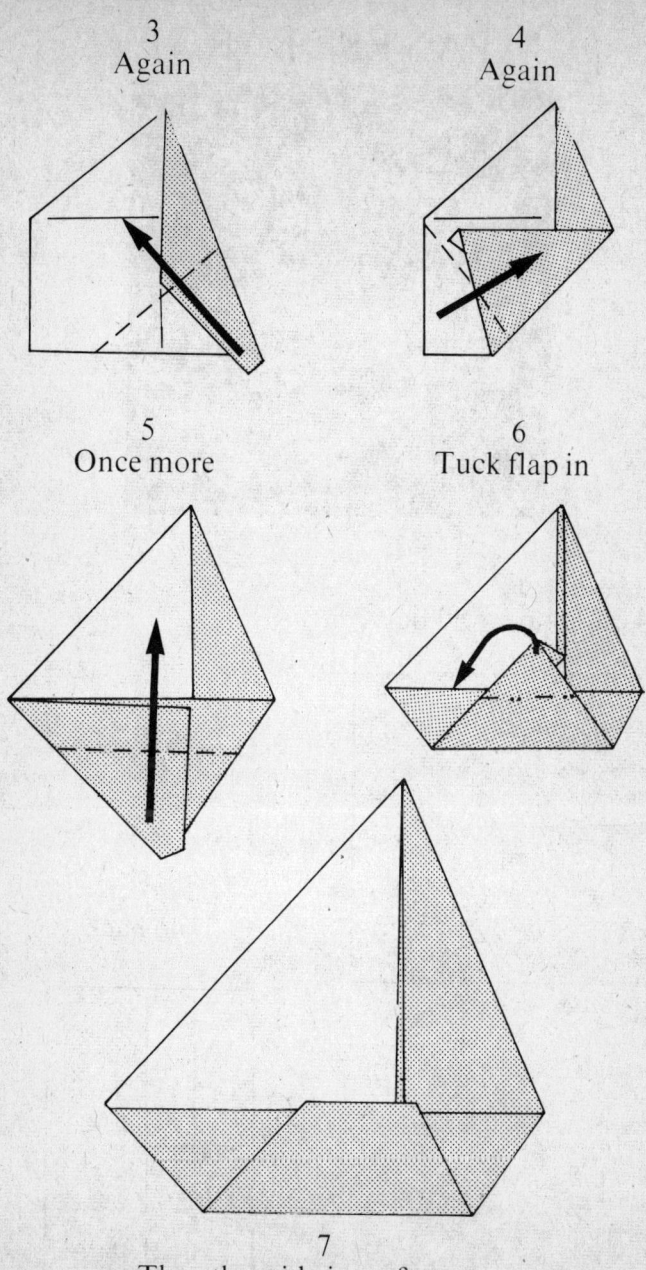

3
Again

4
Again

5
Once more

6
Tuck flap in

7
The other side is perfect too

JAPANESE BARGE

1
Take a square, fold flap $\frac{1}{3}$

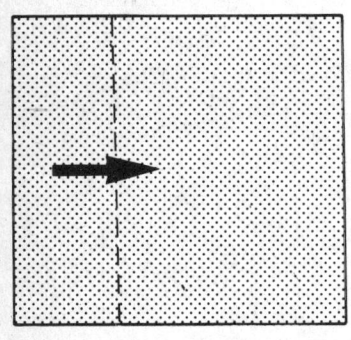

2
Fold back

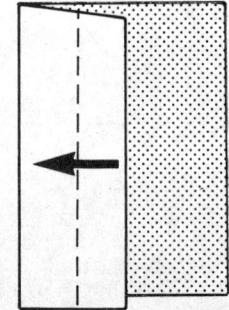

3
Fold flap

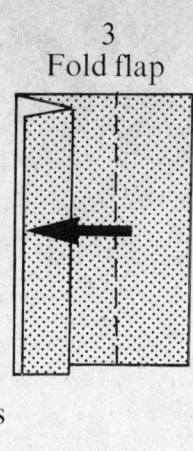

4
Fold 4 corners

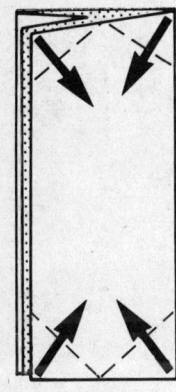

5
Fold flap

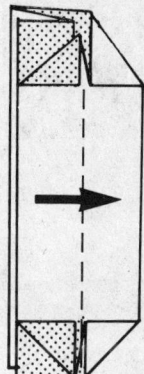

6
Open flap

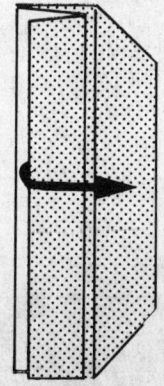

JAPANESE BARGE
(cont.)

7
Fold 4 corners

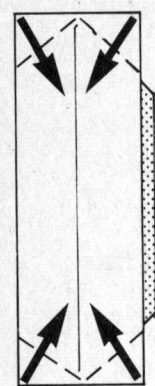

8
Close flap

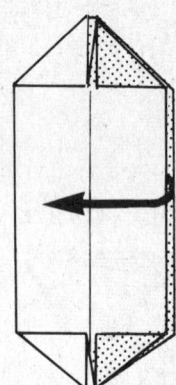

9
Pull sides open

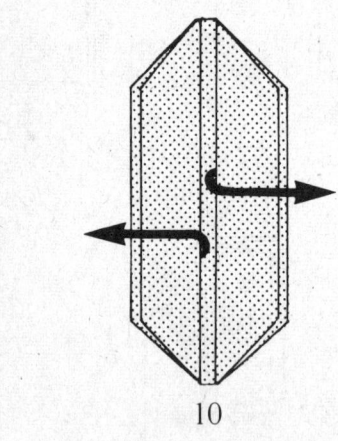

10

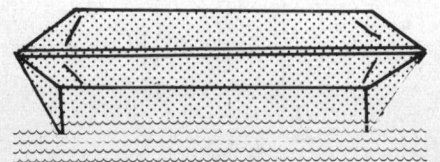

APOLLO 16
by Christopher Swanson
(Leicester)

1
Crease a square to make water bomb base

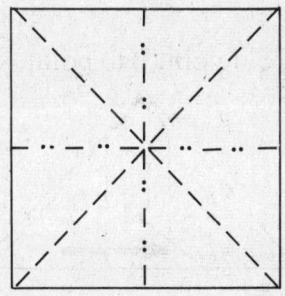

2
Fold point A

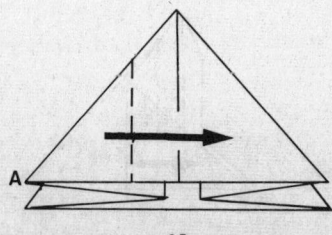

APOLLO 16 (cont.)

3
Fold flap

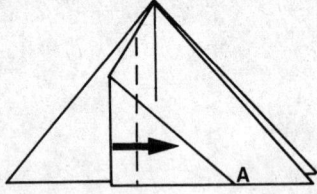

4
Fold edge. Fold A again

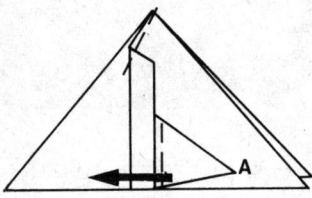

5
Fold point B to point A

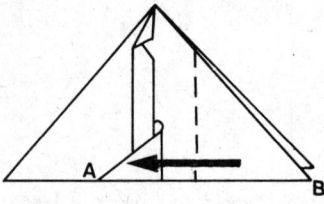

6
Repeat folds 3 and 4

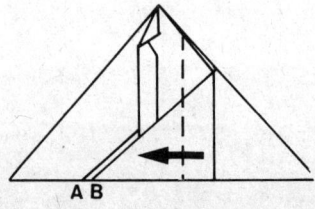

7
Fold A and B in

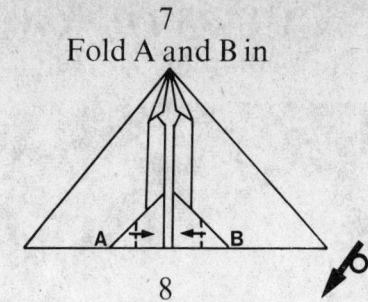

8
Turn over. Repeat all folds for points C and D

9

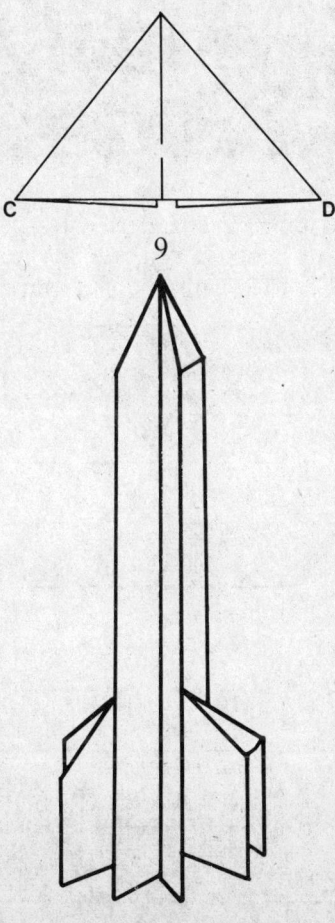

SAILING DINGHY
by Robert Harbin

1
You need 2 squares. First make
the body. Crease diagonal.
Fold corners. Fold flaps

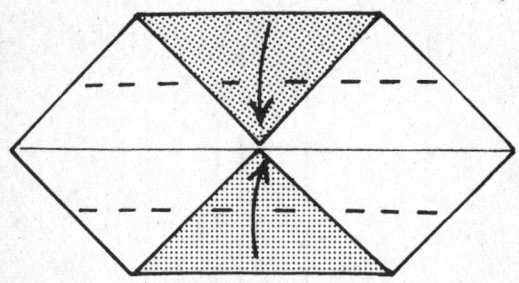

2
Fold in half

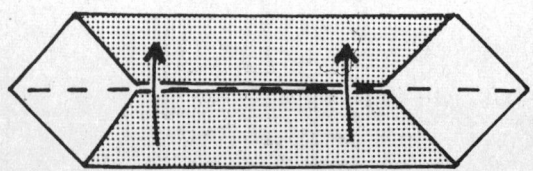

3
Reverse fold points

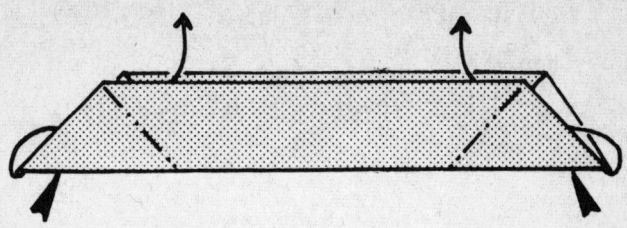

4
Fold points in

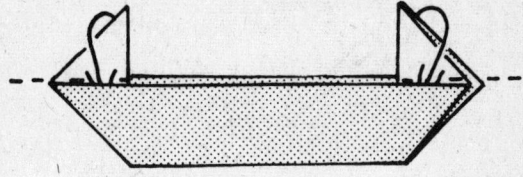

5
And again

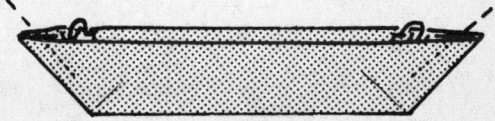

6

7
Take the second square for the sail.
Fold over and over for mast

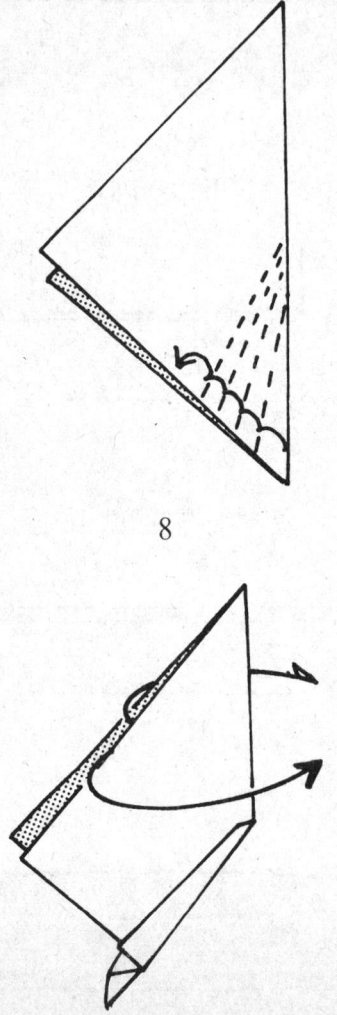

8

9
Inside out

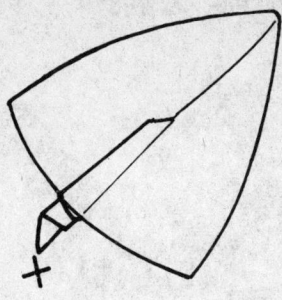

10
Put mast under flap in boat

JAPANESE CUP

1
Take a square and crease.
Fold other diagonal up

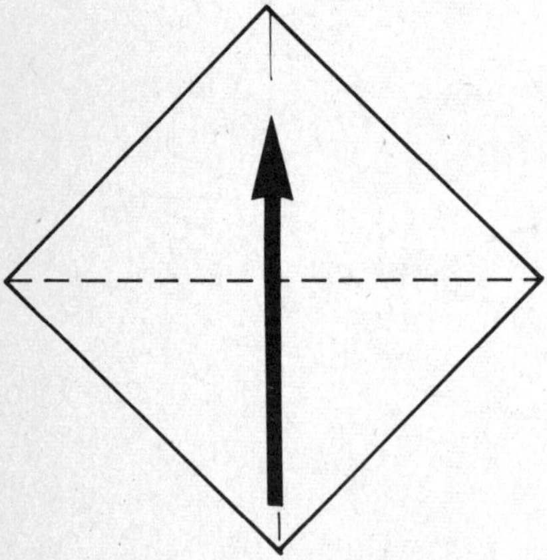

2
Fold A left

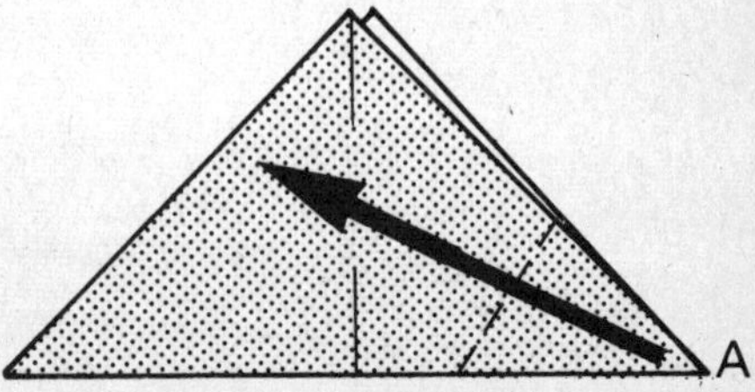

A

3
Fold B right

B

4
Fold flaps down front and behind

5

BAG or HAT
by M. Simpson (New Zealand)

1
Take a rectangle any size.
Fold flap behind

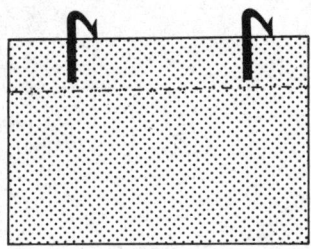

2
Fold sides in

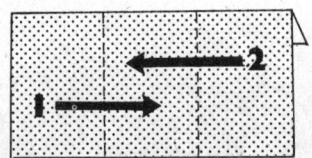

3
Fold A under B

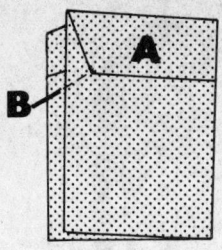

4

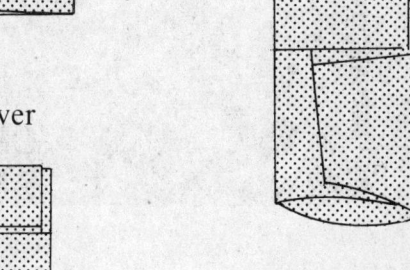

5
Turn over

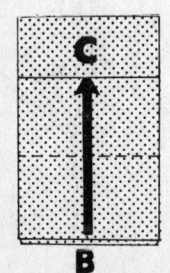

6
Tuck B under C

7

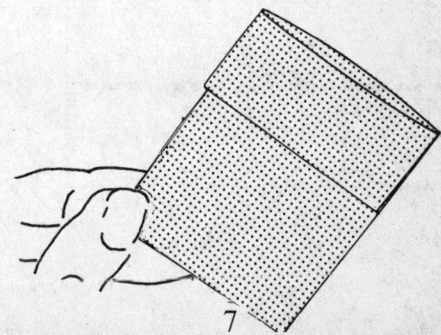

With a sheet of newspaper, you can make a great bag for picnics or a hat for a sunny day

ENVELOPE
by Gillian Dixon (North Shields)

1
Take a square.
Fold 2 corners, fold flaps

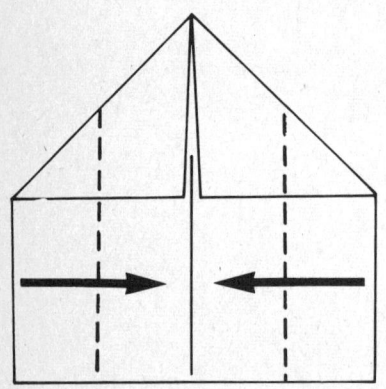

2
Open out and squash

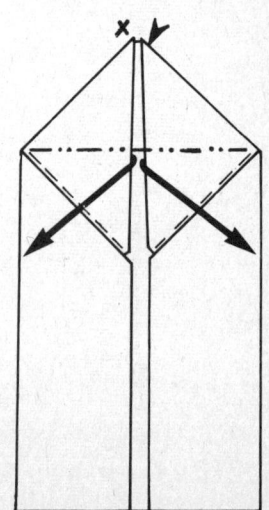

3
Fold bottom corners

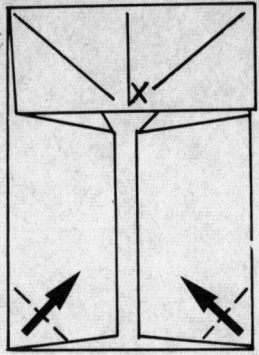

4
Tuck flap into pocket

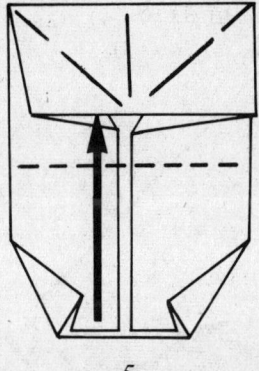

5

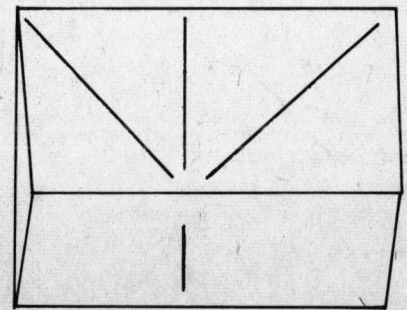

SEE-SAW
by Robert Calder (Aberdeen)

1

Take a square and crease
diagonals. Fold sides in

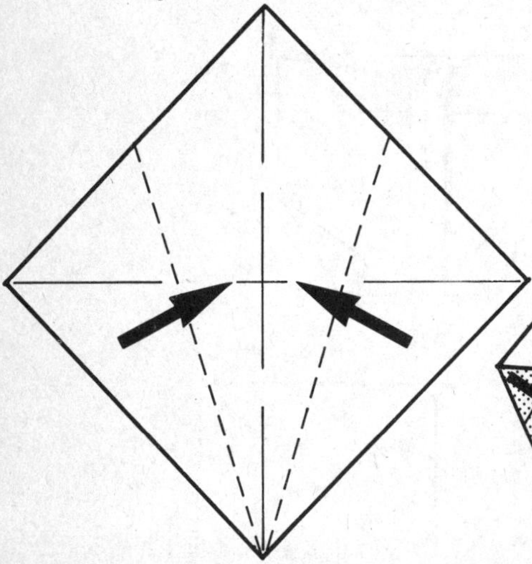

2
Fold sides in

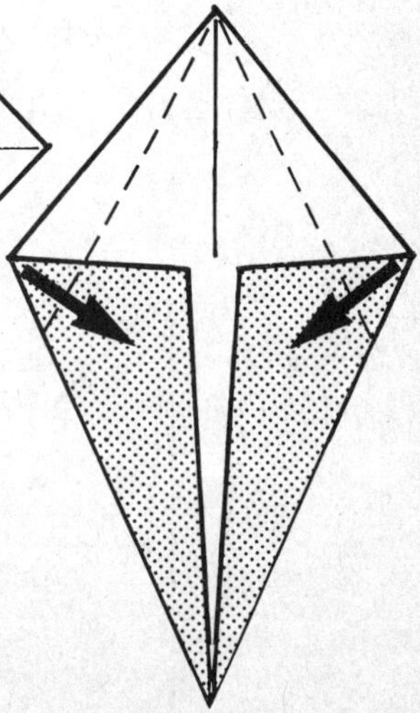

3
Fold sides in. Turn over

4
Fold points up and down

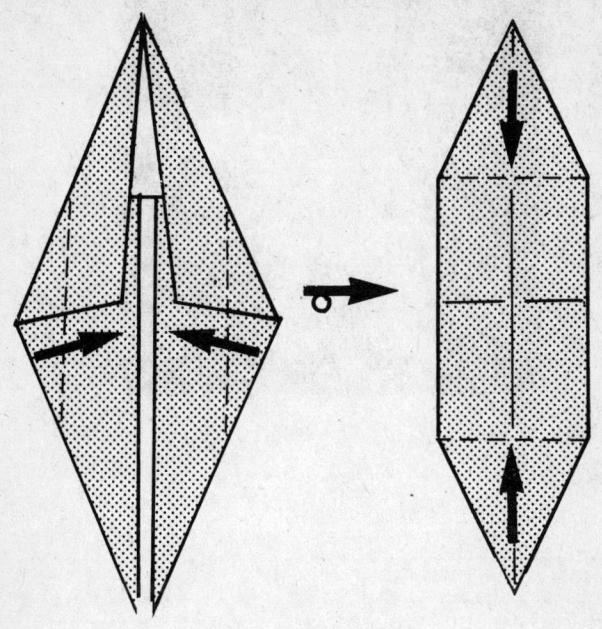

5
Open folds to form see-saw

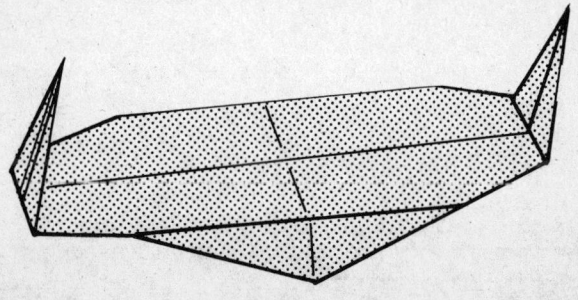

PAPER BONNET
by Linda Smart (Enfield)

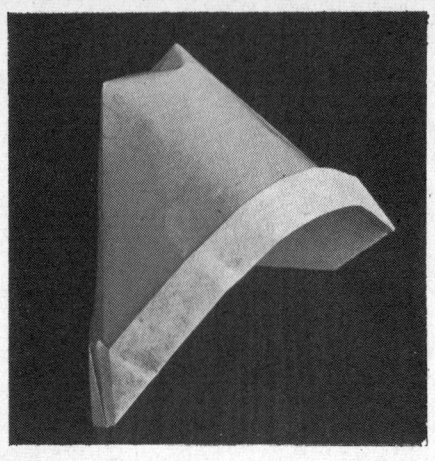

1
Crease a square, fold in half

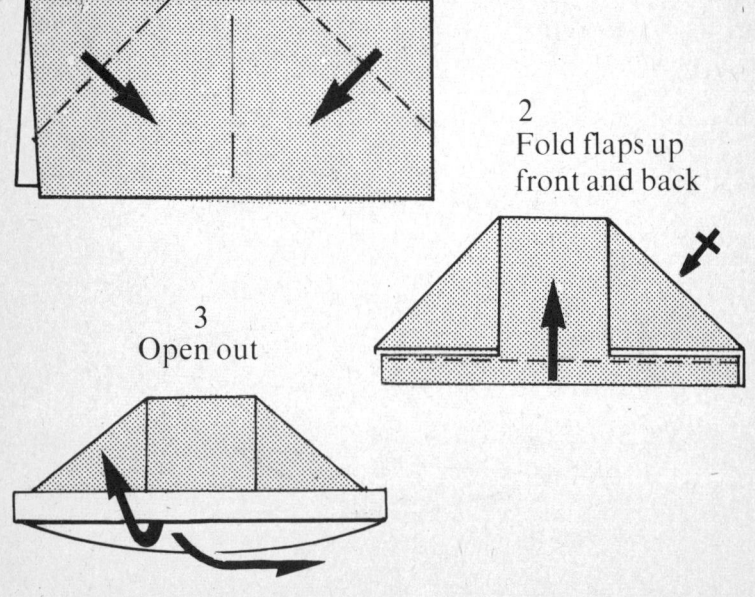

2
Fold flaps up
front and back

3
Open out

80

4
Fold corners

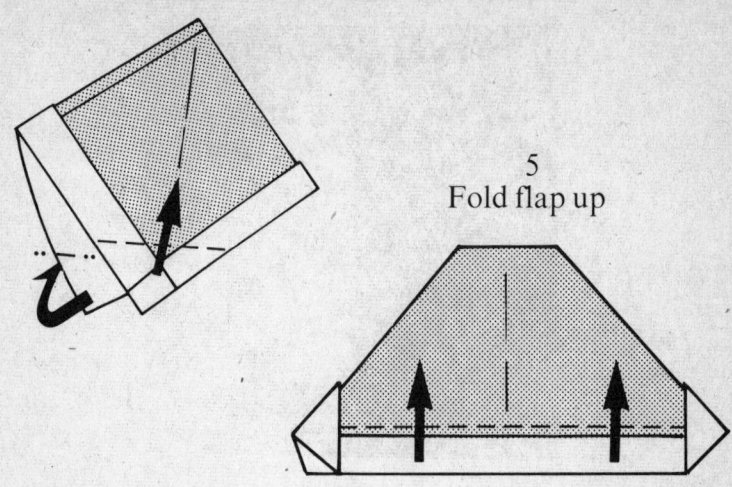

5
Fold flap up

6
Open again, form bonnet

7

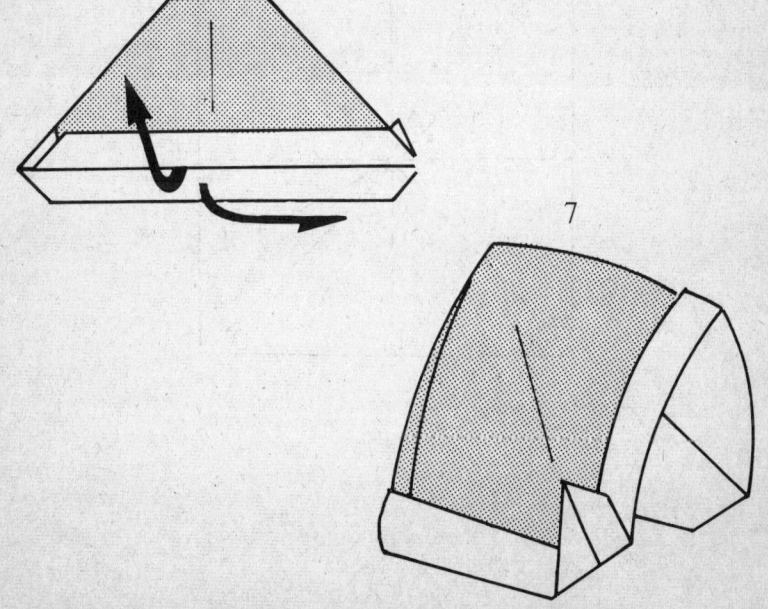

PARTY HAT
by Sharon Brown (Beeston)

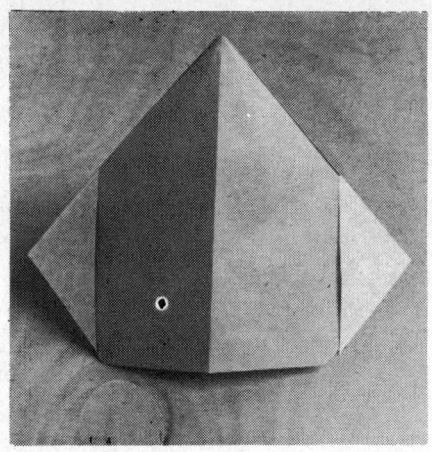

1

Crease a square carefully

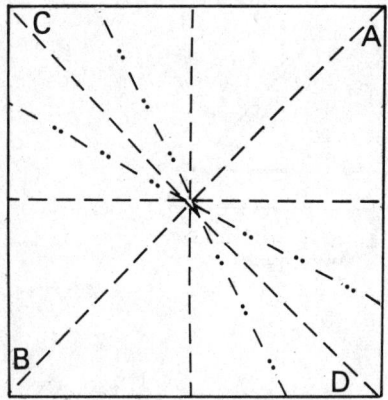

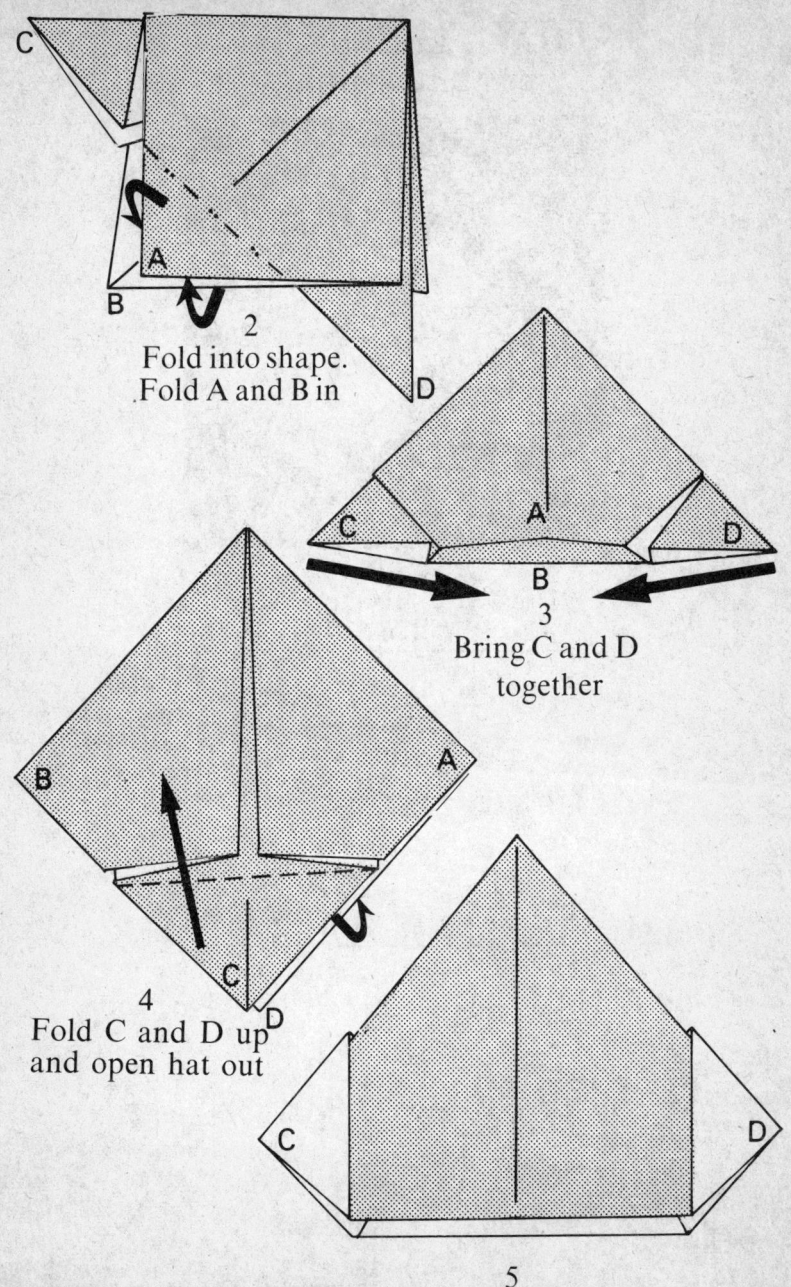

C

2
Fold into shape.
Fold A and B in

B

A

D

C

A

D

B

3
Bring C and D
together

B

A

C

D

4
Fold C and D up
and open hat out

C

D

5

DUTCH BONNET
by Martin Griffett

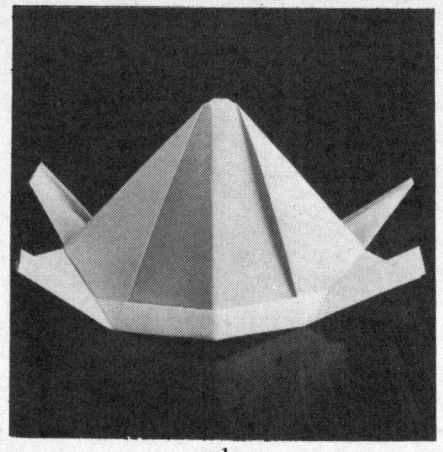

1
Crease a rectangle.
Fold in half

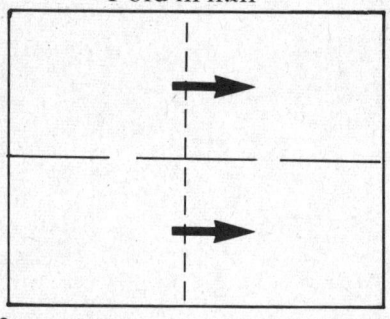

2
Fold A and B and squash

3
Fold flaps behind

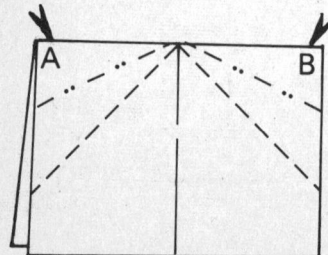

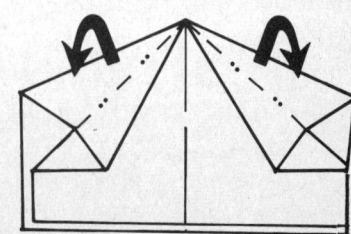

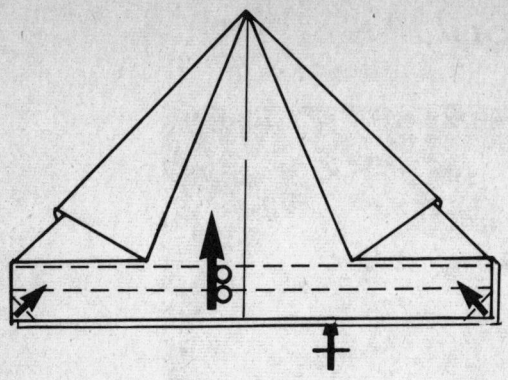

4

Fold little corners and then
fold over and over. Repeat behind

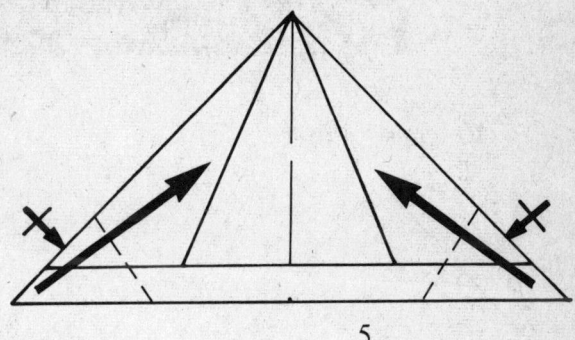

5

Fold points up front and behind

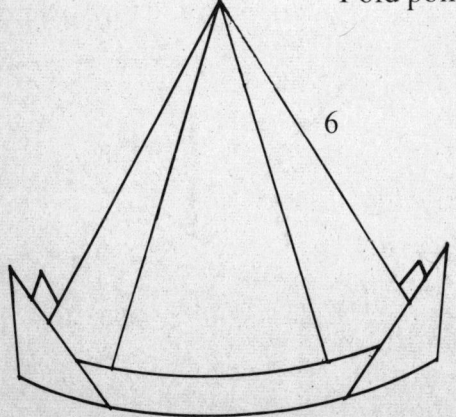

6

BISHOP'S MITRE
by Lucian Dulling (Skipton)

1
Fold a square so

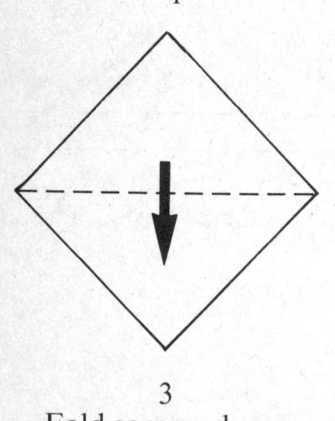

2
Fold flap up and turn over

3
Fold corners down

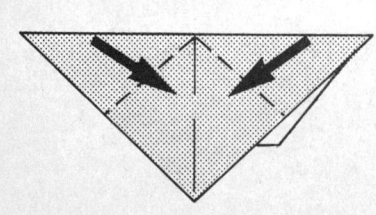

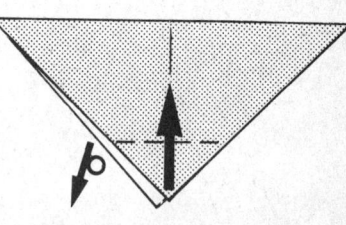

4
Squash fold corners

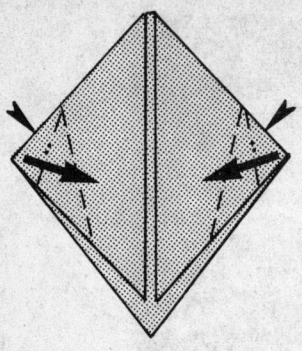

5
Fold flaps up

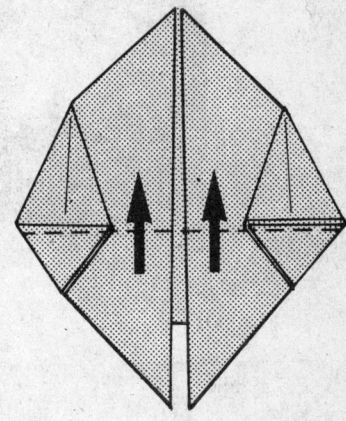

6
Fold flaps up and under

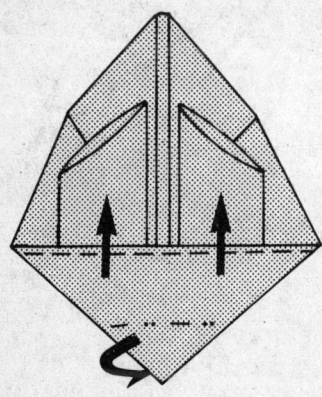

7

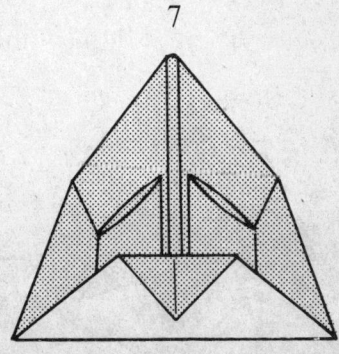

XMAS HAT 1
by Robert Harbin

1
Fold a square so.
Fold A left

2
Fold B right

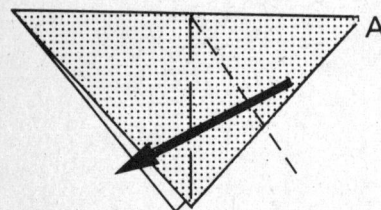

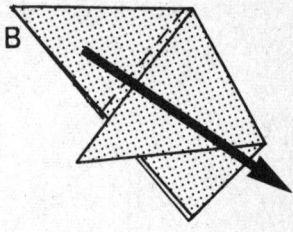

3
Fold 3 flaps up, 1 flap behind

4

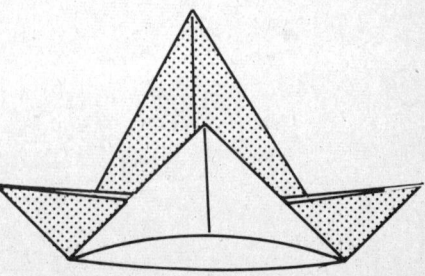

XMAS HAT 2
by Robert Harbin

1
Fold a square so.
Fold flaps in front and
repeat behind.

2
Fold A and B so

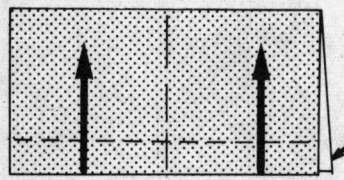
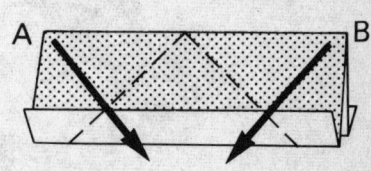

3

4
Fold corners C and D then
fold flaps into hat

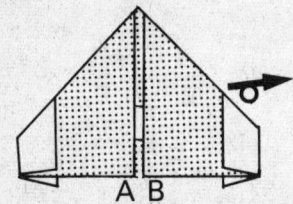
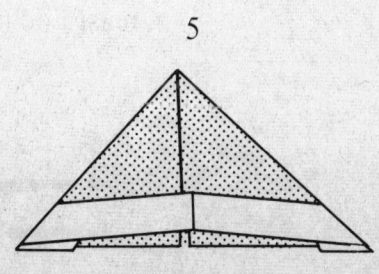

5

NELSON'S HAT
by David Green
(West Wickham)

1

Fold a square along diagonal

2

Crease and unfold

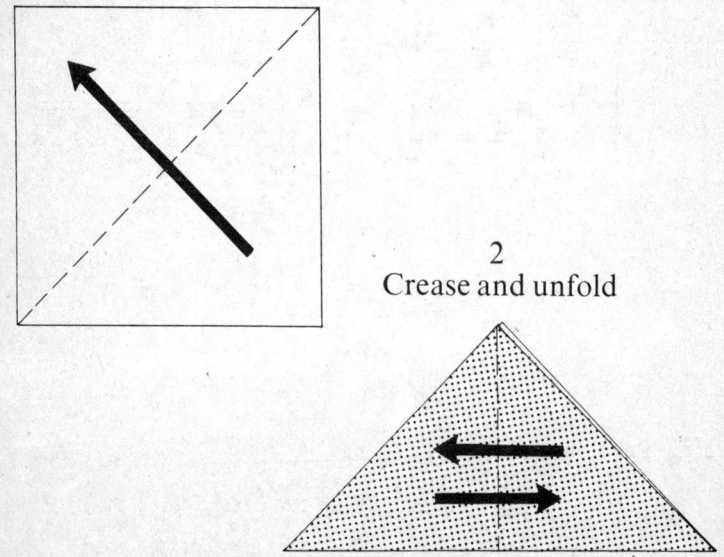

3
Fold points down and unfold

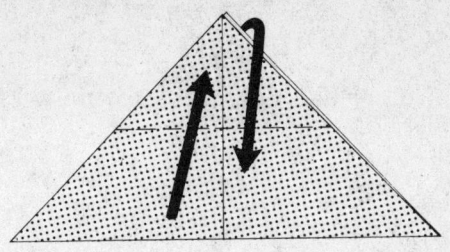

4
Fold points in

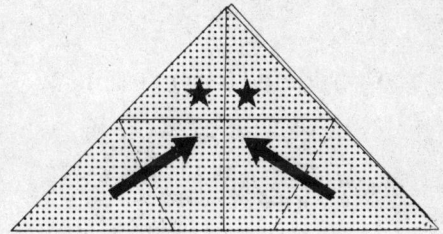

5
Lift points and squash fold

6
Fold points in

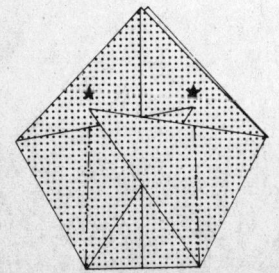
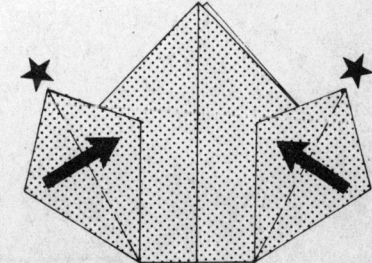

NELSON'S HAT
(cont.)

7
Fold other flaps down

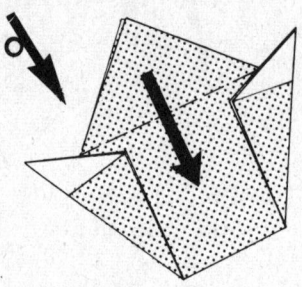

8
Fold one flap in front

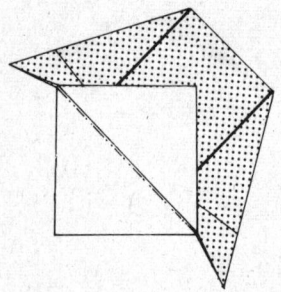

9
If you use a large enough piece of paper you can actually wear it too!

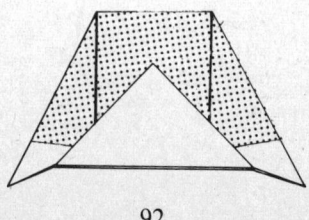

SANTA CLAUS
by Robert Harbin

1

Take a square of paper, red one side.
Fold 3 corners in

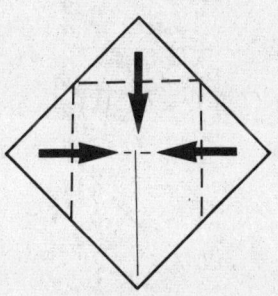

2

Fold over and over

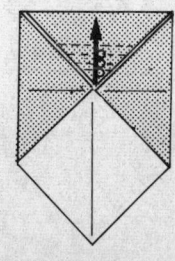

SANTA CLAUS (cont.)

3
Fold flaps out

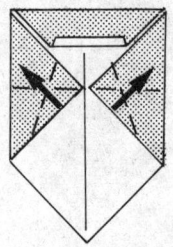

4
Fold flaps behind

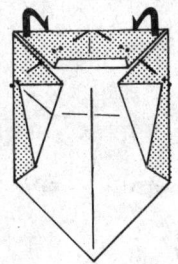

5
Fold in half, pull hat out

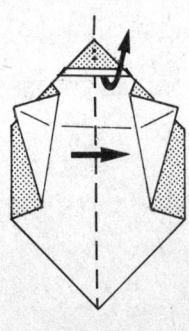

6
Fold flaps.

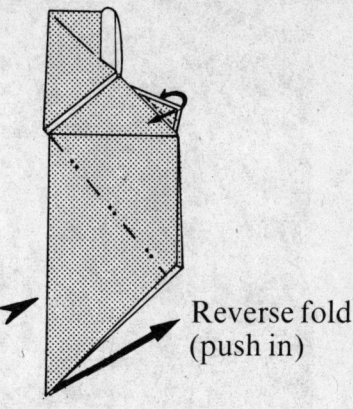

Reverse fold
(push in)

7
Form feet by reverse
folding twice

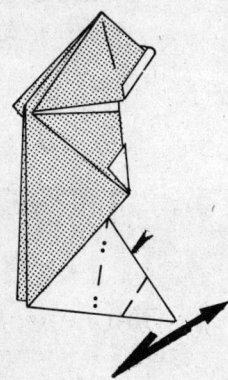

7a
So

8

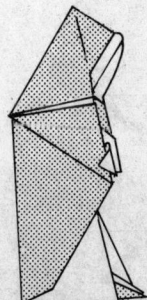

TIE
by T. Oram (Liverpool)

1

Take a rectangle 10 × 18cm.
Crease middle line, make crimp

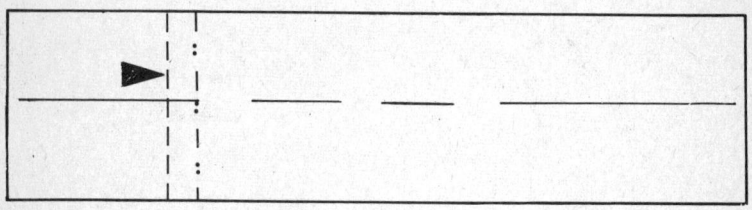

2

Fold flaps, squash 2 corners. Turn upright

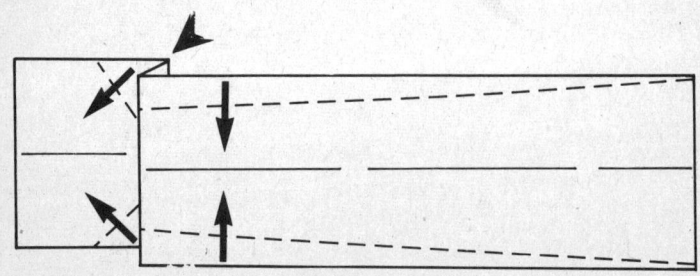

3
Fold 4 corners

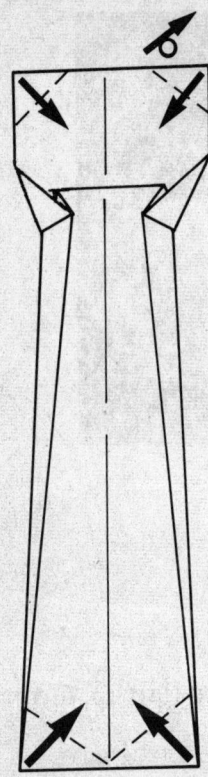

4

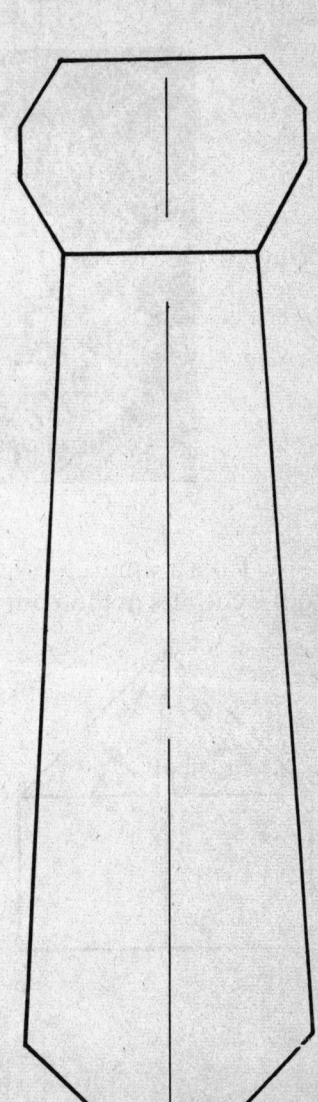

JAPANESE GENTLEMAN
by Christopher Dolphin
(Tamworth)

1
Take a square.
Fold 2 corners in then out

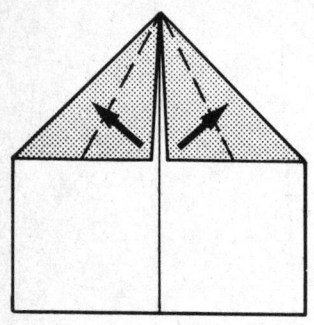

2
Fold flap up, turn over

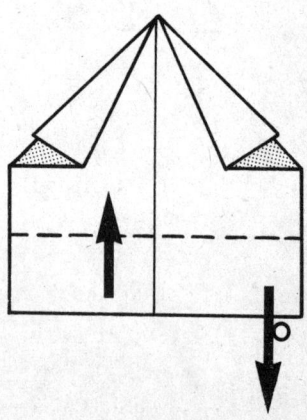

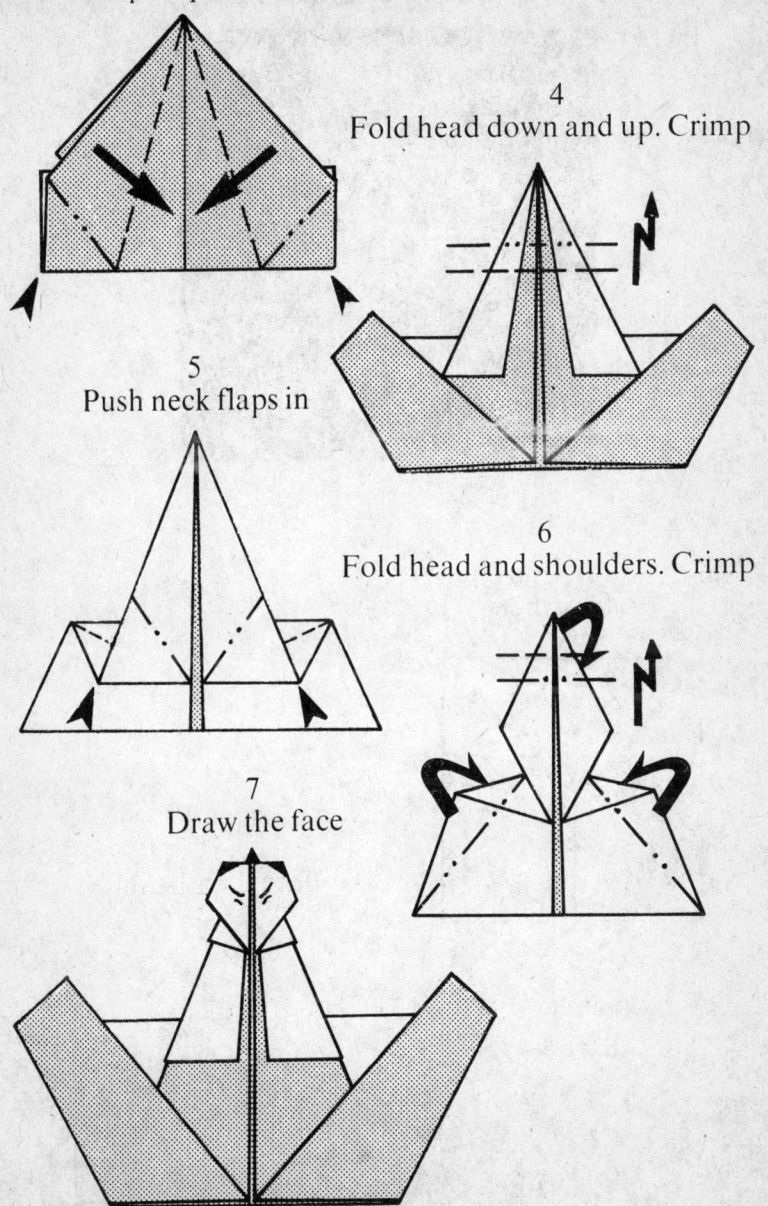

3
Fold flaps, squash corners

4
Fold head down and up. Crimp

5
Push neck flaps in

6
Fold head and shoulders. Crimp

7
Draw the face

BOOK-MARK
by William Chebib (Osterley)

1
Take a square and crease.
Fold corners

2
Fold flaps behind

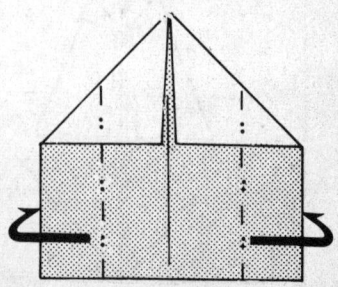

3
Follow X

4
And again

5
Fold flaps behind

6

CONCORDE
by Paul Streeter (Somerset)

1
Fold a square so.
Fold flap in

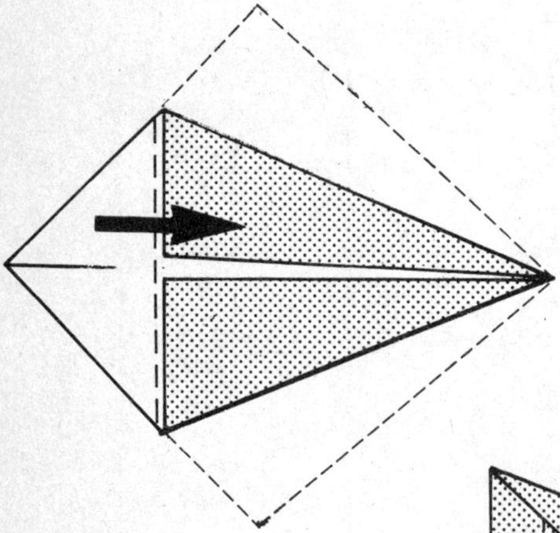

2
Fold point in.
Fold flap out

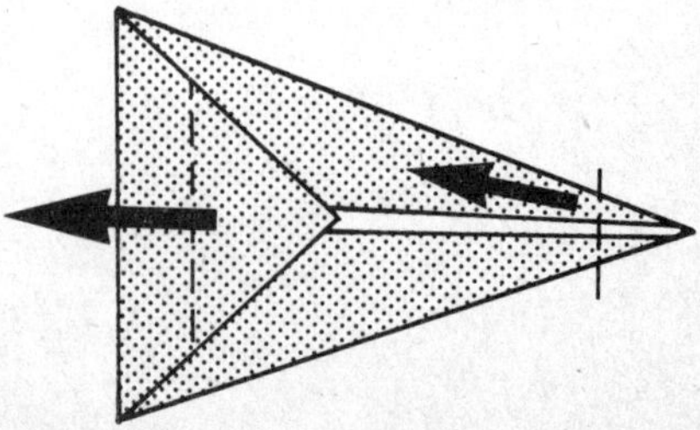

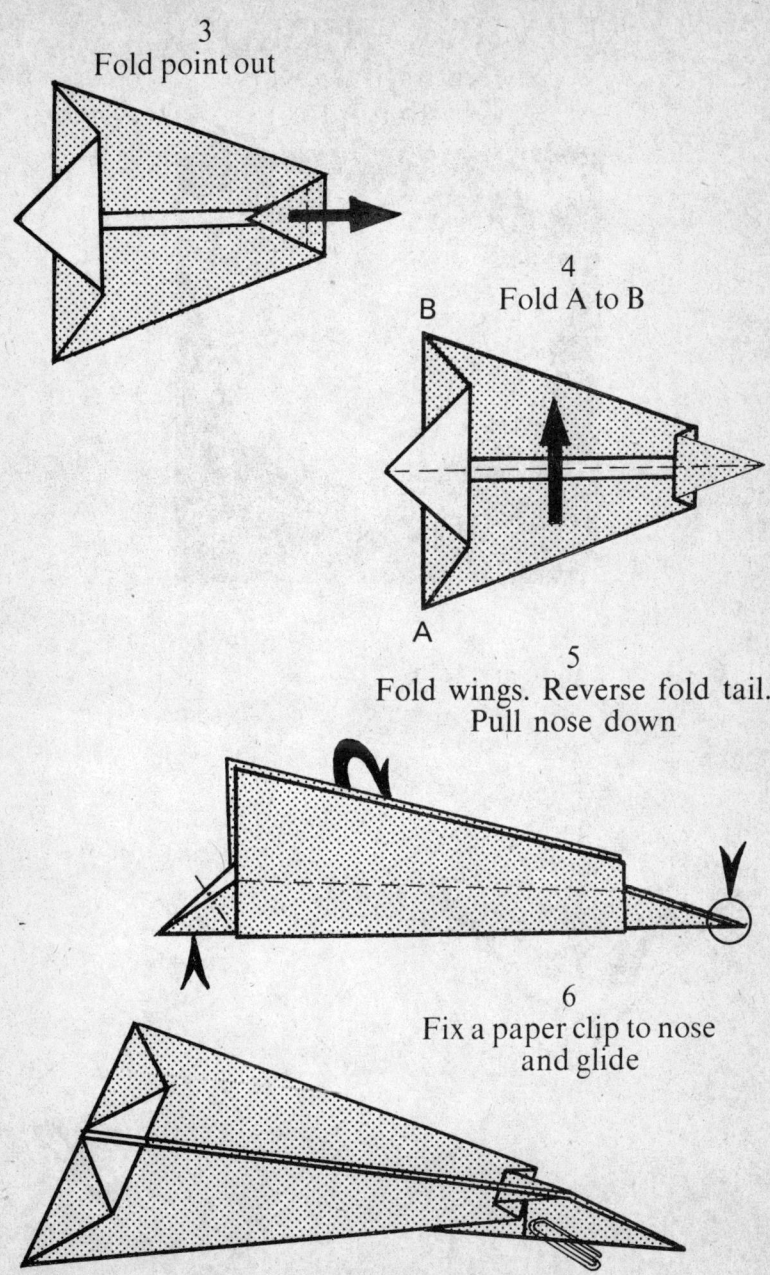

3
Fold point out

4
Fold A to B

B

A

5
Fold wings. Reverse fold tail.
Pull nose down

6
Fix a paper clip to nose
and glide

SERVIETTE HOLDER
by Kathryn Brewer
(Northampton)

1
Crease a square and fold

2
Crease well and sink

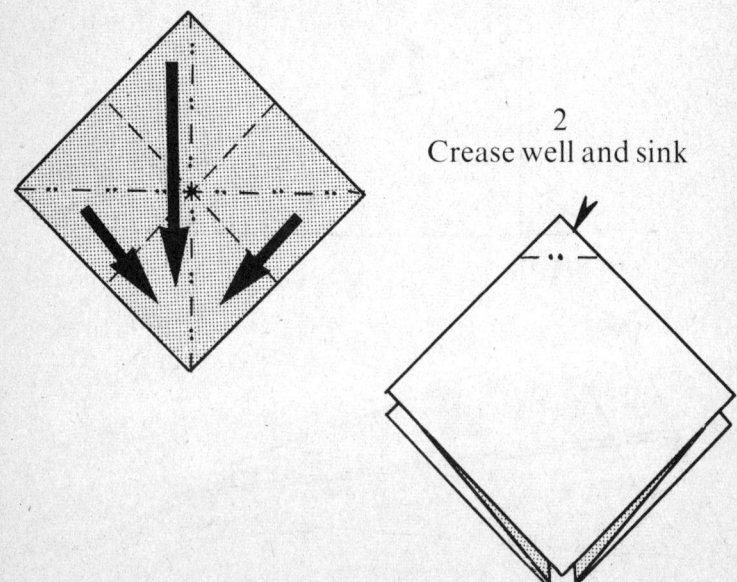

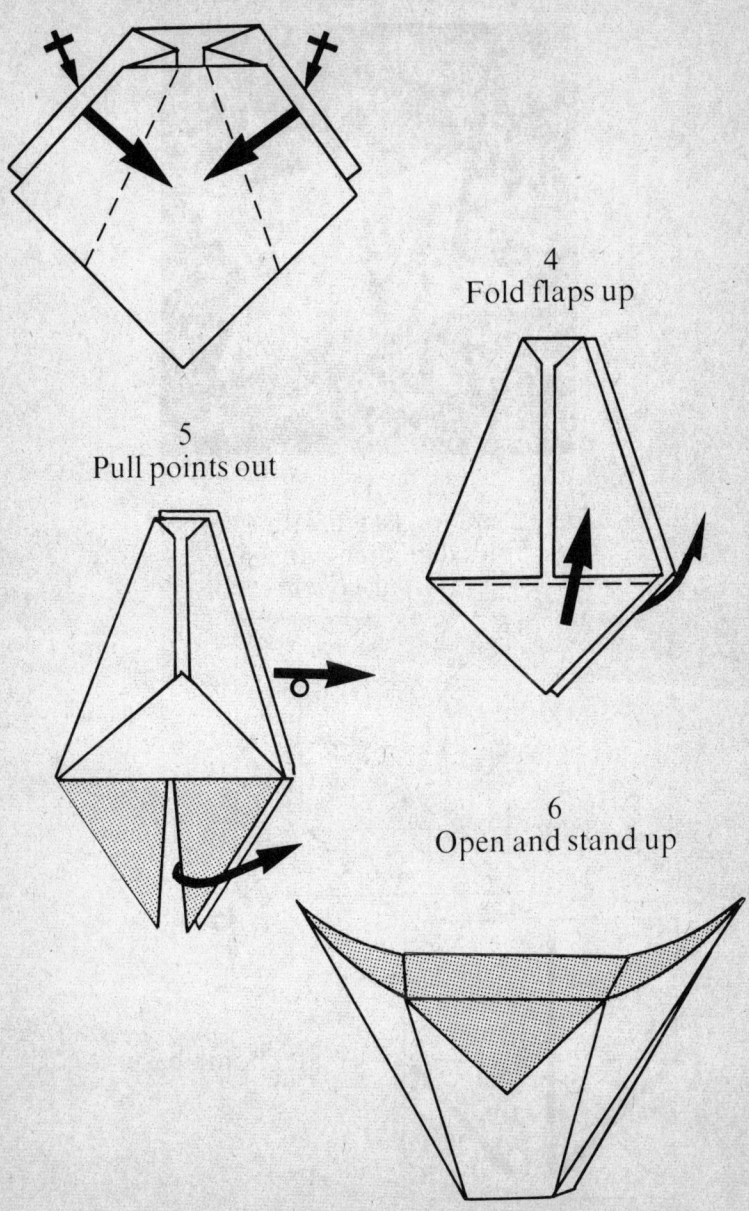

3
Fold sides in front and back

4
Fold flaps up

5
Pull points out

6
Open and stand up

105

U.F.O.
by Stephen Lawson (Darlington)

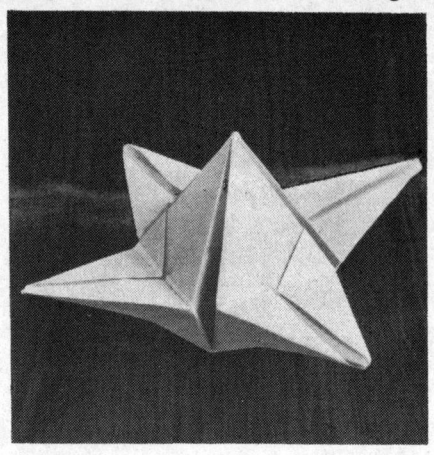

1
Take a square. Begin with 4 corners
folded in, then out again.
Turn over

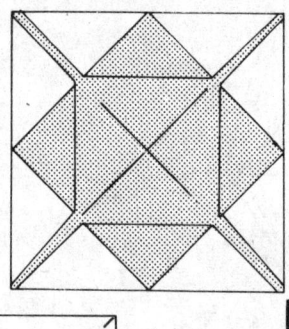

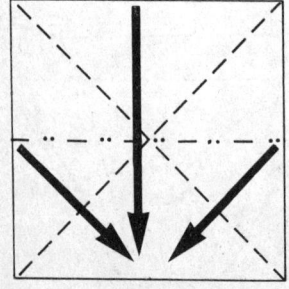

2
Water bomb base

106

3
Squash fold 4 points

4
Petal fold 4 points

5
Pull 4 points halfway down

6
Hold U.F.O. by one wing and spin away from you. It lands on its 'feet'

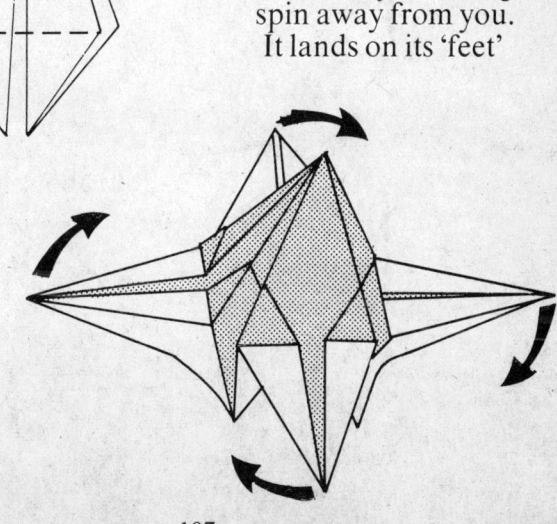

BOBSLEIGH
by Jonathan Smith
(Wath-upon-Dearne)

1
Take a square.
Crease then fold corners in

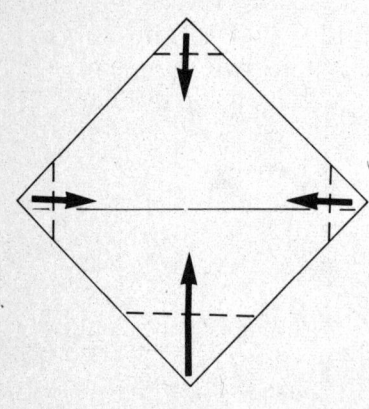

2
Fold above and below

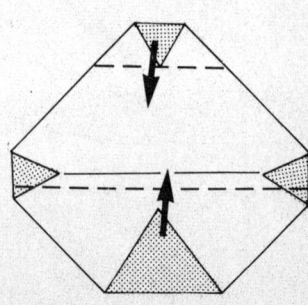

3
Turn over

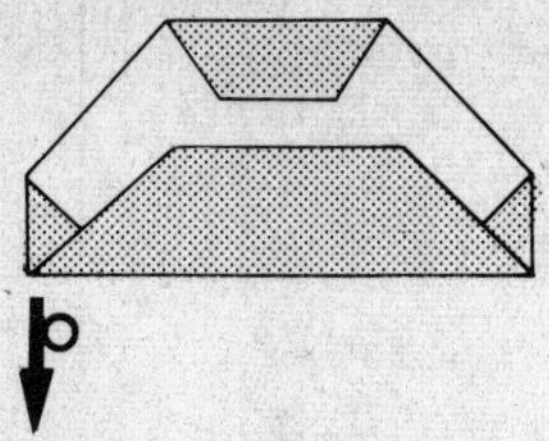

4
Fold $\frac{1}{3}$ left

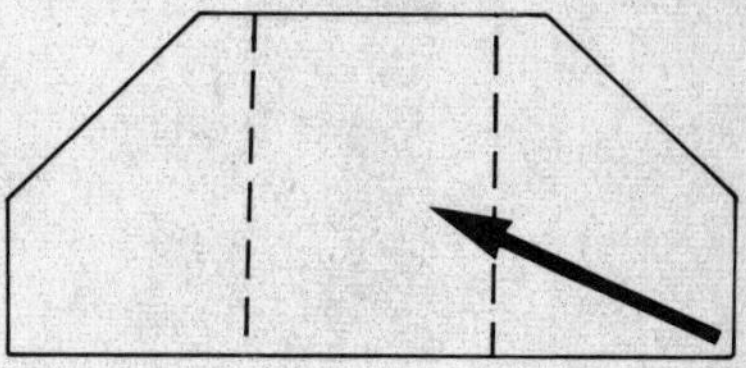

5
Fold flap into pocket

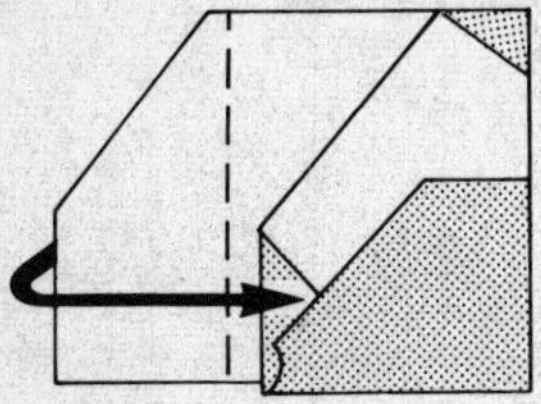

6
Turn over so

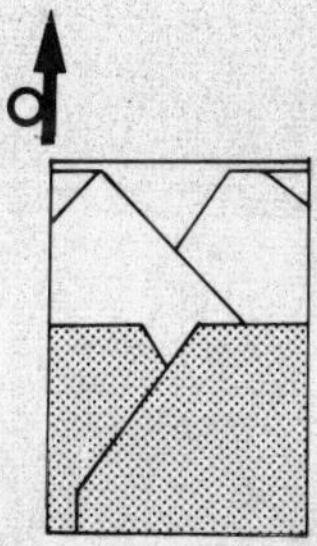

7
Push corners in at foot of bobsleigh, then open bobsleigh

8

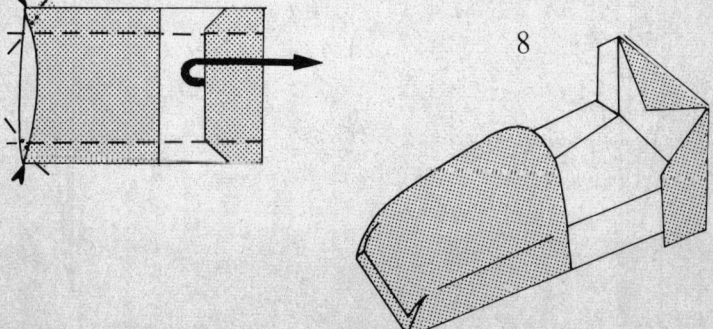

TUTANKHAMEN
by Deborah Holmes (Sedgley)

1
A creased square, sides folded
in, and again

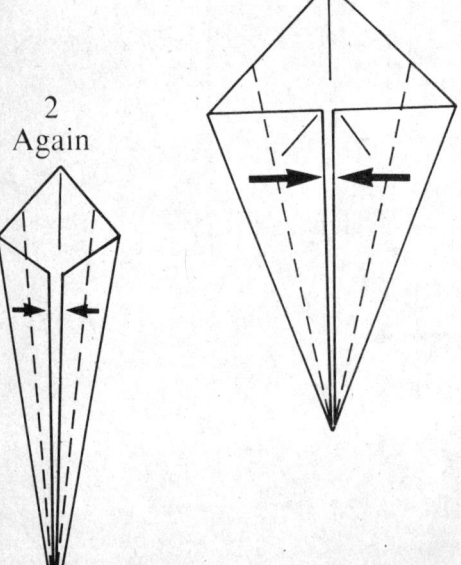

2
Again

3
Fold flaps out

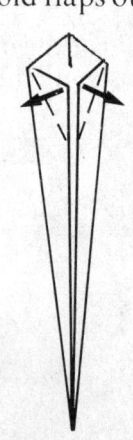

4
Crimp head. Fold behind. Crimp base

5
Now decorate in colour

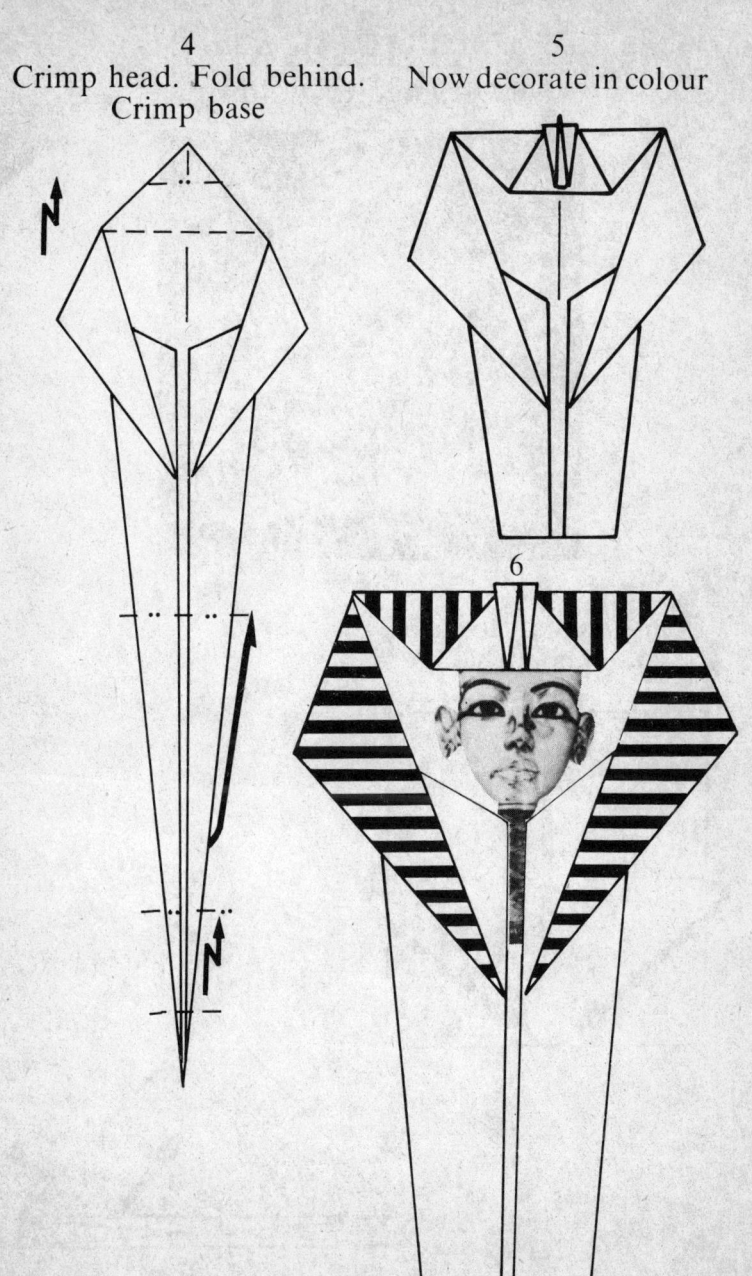

6

CATHEDRAL
by Alison Reynolds

1
Crease a square to make
water bomb base

2
Lift 2 corners and squash

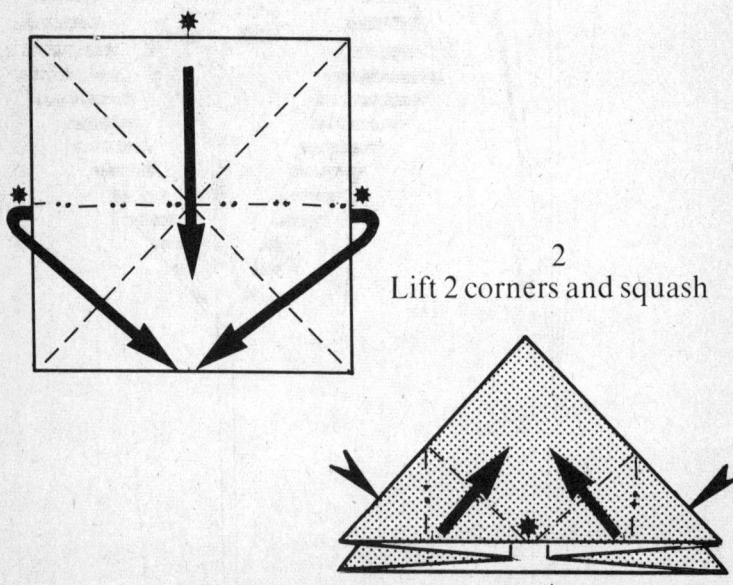

3
Fold A and B under

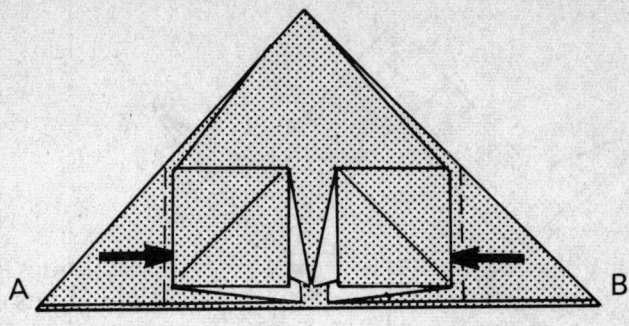

A   B

4
Lift flaps and make petal folds

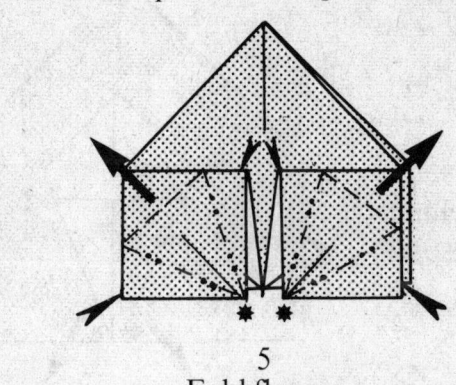

5
Fold flap up

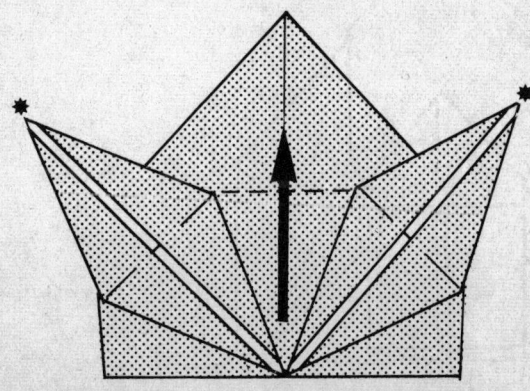

CATHEDRAL (cont.)

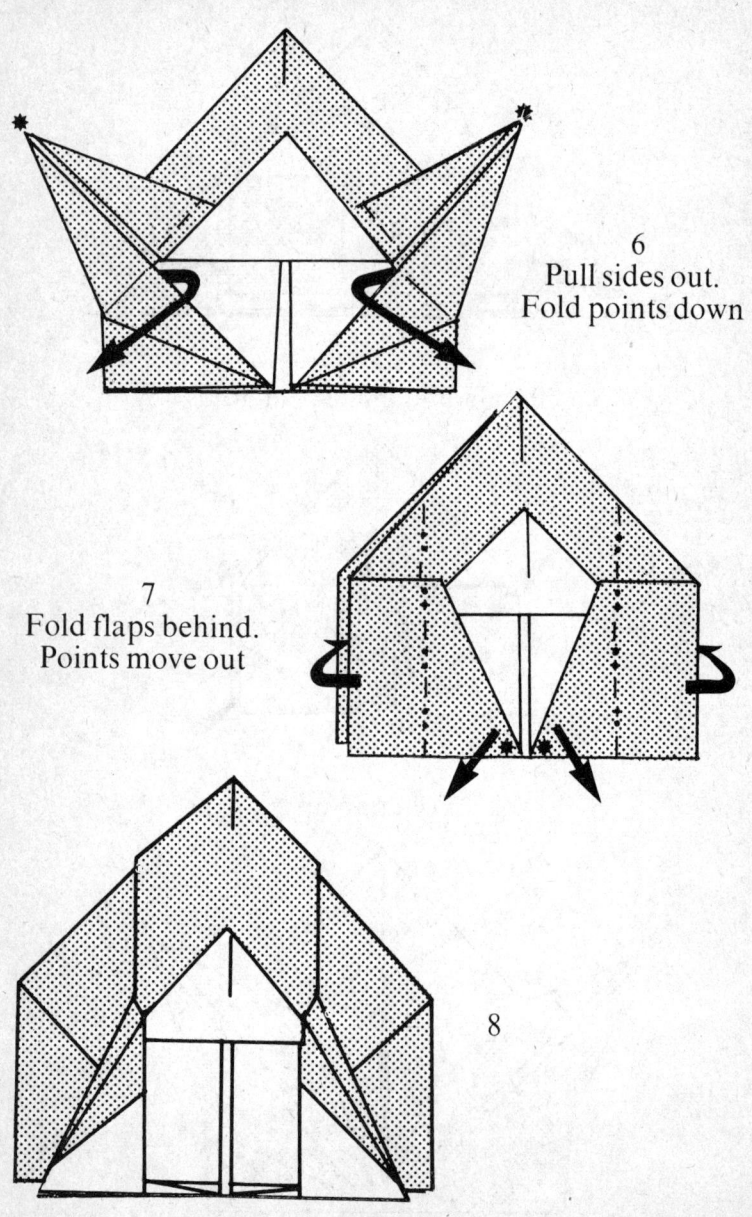

6
Pull sides out.
Fold points down

7
Fold flaps behind.
Points move out

8

PIN-UP PICTURE FRAME
by Mary Cartwright
(Kidderminster)

1
Take a square
fold sides in to centre

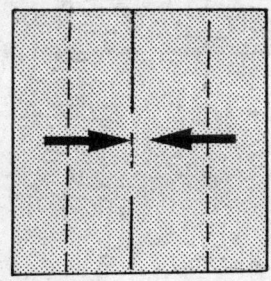

2
And again

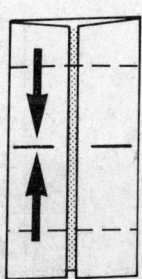

PIN-UP PICTURE
FRAME
(cont.)

3
Crease and pull corners out

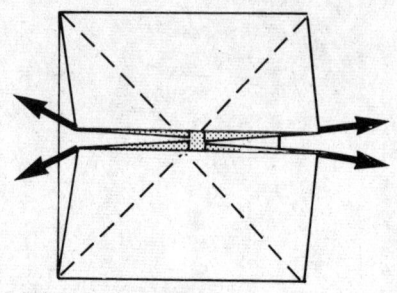

4
Lift and squash 4 points

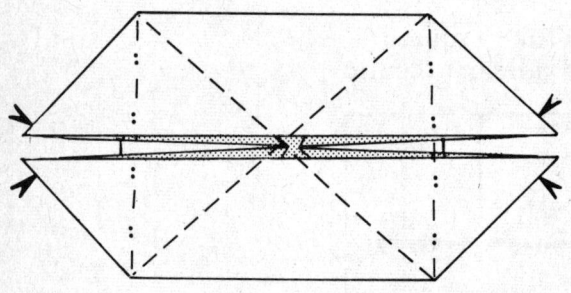

5
Fold flaps out

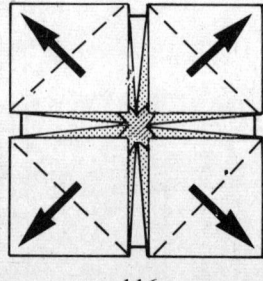

6
Put photo inside and fold
4 flaps under

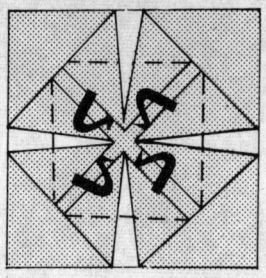

7

SPANISH DECORATION

1
Crease diagonals on a square.
Fold 4 corners in

2
Pleat each flap by folding
8 times

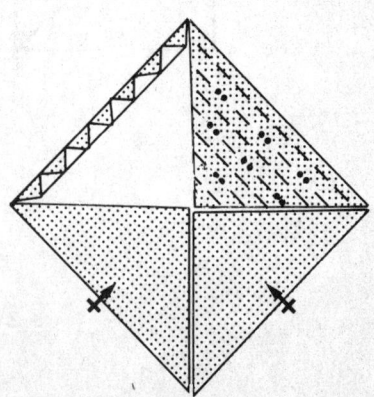

3
Turn over

4
Fold 4 corners in

5

WATER FLOWER
by Catherine Plant
(Willenhall)

1
Take a square. Start with
corners—fold in.
Fold each new corner behind

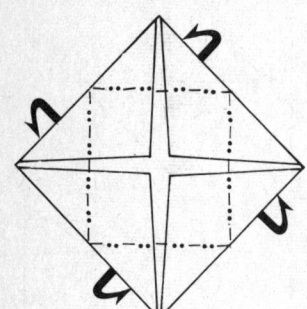

2
Fold 4 times

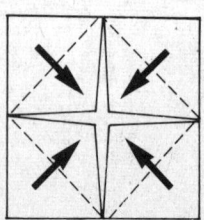

3

Turn over

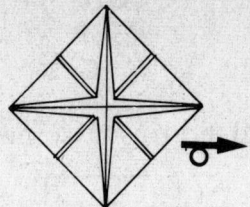

4

Open each out

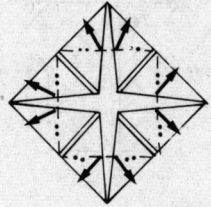

5

Turn over

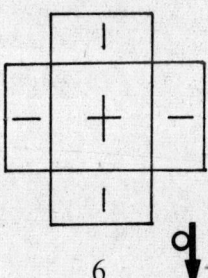

6

Open out 4 times.
Fold 4 small corners

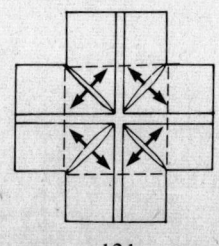

WATER FLOWER
(cont.)

7
Fold the 4 inside corners out

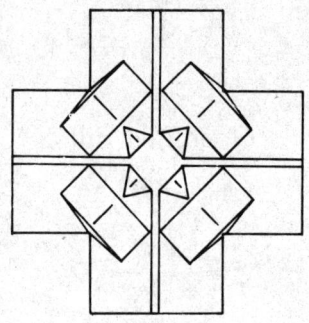

WATER LILY
by Robert Harbin

1
Crease diagonals on a square.
Fold corners in

2
Fold corners in

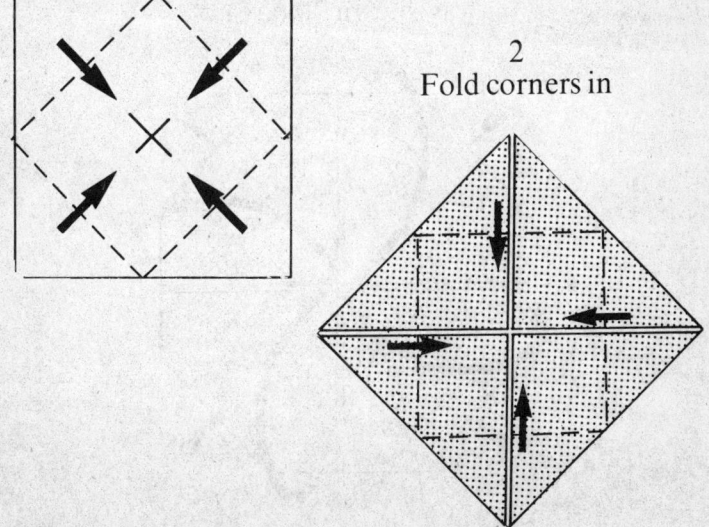

WATER LILY
(cont.)

3
Fold corners behind

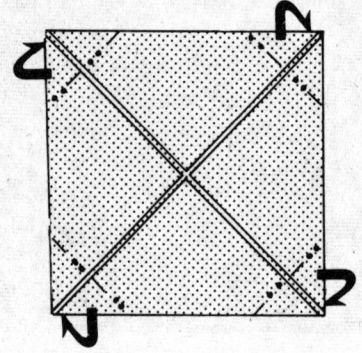

4
Turn 4 flaps inside out
as shown (No. 5)

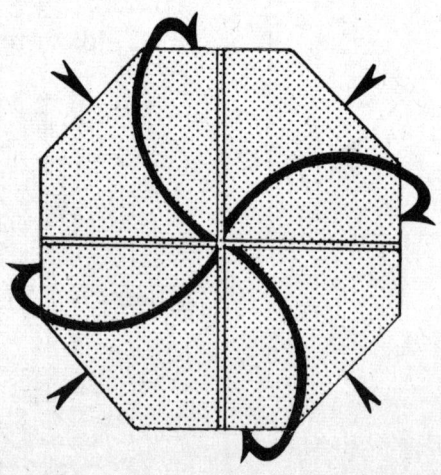

5
Grip with fingers,
turn inside out with thumbs

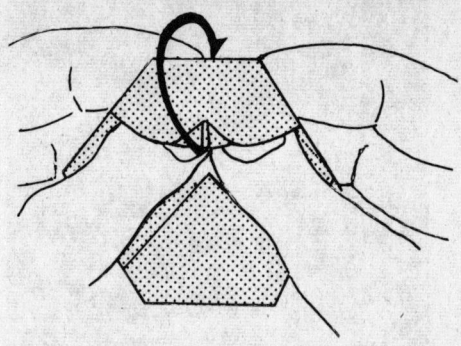

6
Fold petals out

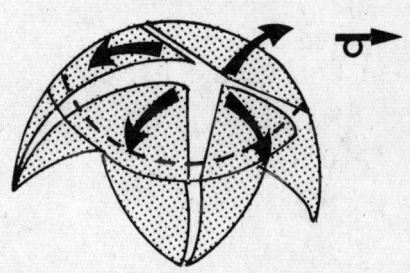

7
Put a gift inside

PRAYING LADY
by Andrew Tuft (Oldham)

1
Take a square. Crease diagonal,
fold sides in. Fold behind

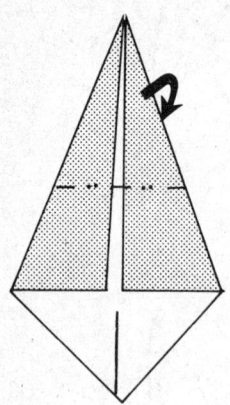

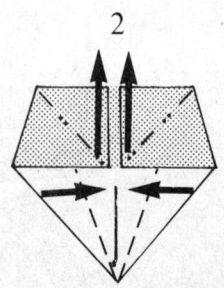

126

3
The fish base

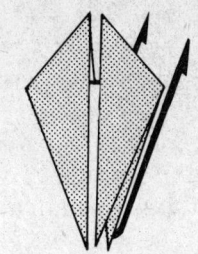

4

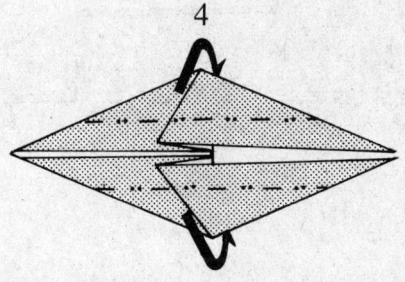

5
Fold point in—pull points out

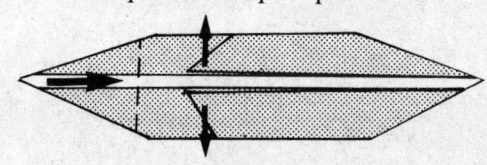

6
Fold in half

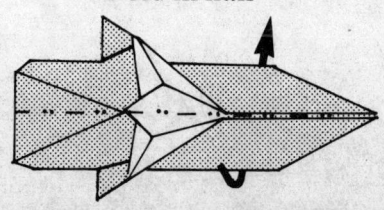

PRAYING LADY (cont.)

7
Make 3 reverse folds
at base and head

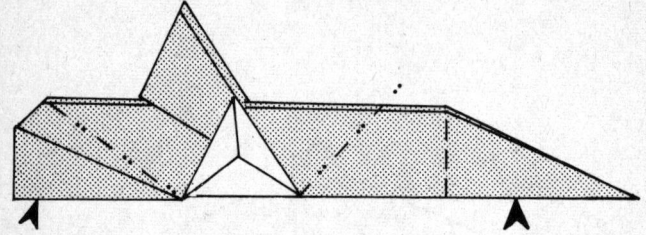

8

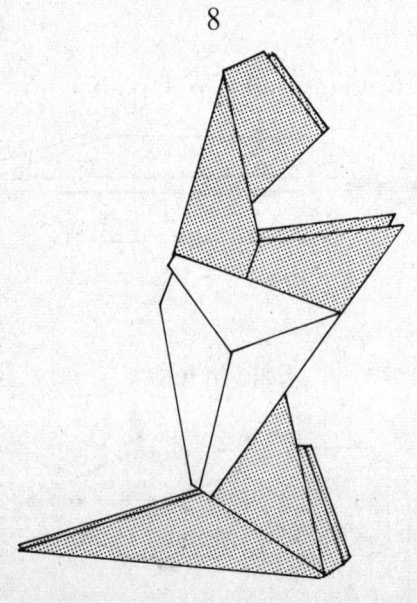